Praise for *Rigor by Design, Not Chance*

Karin Hess's book is a must for anyone incorporating rigor in their classrooms and schools. She balances research-based content with practical examples to ensure classroom implementation. If you are implementing rigor in your classroom, this is a great addition to your library.

—Dr. Barbara Blackburn, author of numerous books,
including *Rigor Is Not a Four-Letter Word*

Karin Hess brings as sharp a lens as I have ever seen to student understanding, assessment, and engagement. She brings rare and illuminating precision to the structure and language of classroom assessment practices. It would be impossible to read this book and not become a better teacher—right away.

—Ron Berger, senior advisor,
Teaching & Learning, EL Education

Karin Hess has written a well-researched and valuable book on strategies to help teachers purposefully incorporate much-needed rigor into teaching and learning. This must-have book is rich with practical brain-friendly suggestions that promote student engagement to make learning meaningful and enjoyable.

—Dr. David Sousa, author of more than 20 books,
including *How the Brain Learns* and *Brain-Friendly Assessments*

With the clarity of a long-time practitioner, Hess shares the principles and practices needed for shifting traditional K–12 pedagogy toward the deeper learning students need to become lifelong learners and successful adults. Educators need the mindsets and tools to dig into this challenging work. The book provides compelling rationales, explains essential teacher moves, and offers dozens of strategies to put them into practice. It's an outstanding text for teacher preparation programs or professional learning communities.

—Eliot Levine, research director, Aurora Institute, and author
of *One Kid at a Time: Big Lessons from a Small School*

RIGOR BY DESIGN

NOT CHANCE

RIGOR
BY DESIGN
NOT CHANCE

Deeper
Thinking Through
Actionable
Instruction
and Assessment

KARIN
HESS

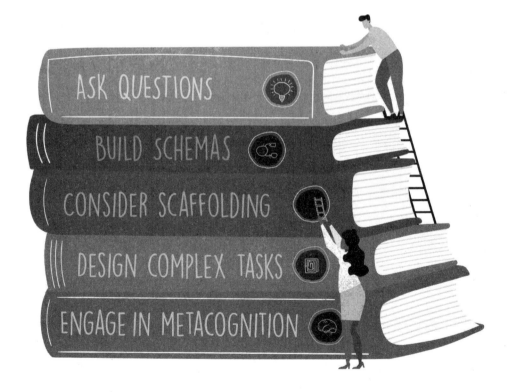

ASK QUESTIONS

BUILD SCHEMAS

CONSIDER SCAFFOLDING

DESIGN COMPLEX TASKS

ENGAGE IN METACOGNITION

ascd

Arlington, Virginia USA

2800 Shirlington Road, Suite 1001 • Arlington, VA 22206 USA
Phone: 1-800-933-2723 or 1-703-578-9600 • Fax: 1-703-575-5400
Website: www.ascd.org • Email: member@ascd.org
Author guidelines: www.ascd.org/write

Penny Reinart, *Deputy Executive Officer;* Genny Ostertag, *Managing Director, Book Acquisitions & Editing;* Susan Hills, *Senior Acquisitions Editor;* Mary Beth Nielsen, *Editor;* Thomas Lytle, *Creative Director;* Donald Ely, *Art Director;* Marzia Motta/The Hatcher Group, *Graphic Designer;* Valerie Younkin, *Senior Production Designer;* Kelly Marshall, *Production Manager;* Shajuan Martin, *E-Publishing Specialist*

PAPERBACK ISBN: 978-1-4166-3164-4   ASCD product #122036   2/23

PDF E-BOOK ISBN: 978-1-4166-3165-1; see Books in Print for other formats.

Quantity discounts are available: email programteam@ascd.org or call 1-800-933-2723, ext. 5773, or 1-703-575-5773. For desk copies, go to www.ascd.org/deskcopy.

Library of Congress Cataloging-in-Publication Data
Names: Hess, Karin (Karin K.) author.
Title: Rigor by design, not chance : deeper thinking through actionable instruction and assessment / Karin Hess.
Description: Arlington, Virginia : ASCD, [2023] | Includes bibliographical references and index.
Identifiers: LCCN 2022039692 (print) | LCCN 2022039693 (ebook) | ISBN 9781416631644 (paperback) | ISBN 9781416631651 (pdf)
Subjects: LCSH: Cognitive learning. | Thought and thinking—Study and teaching. | Educational tests and measurements. | Motivation in education.
Classification: LCC LB1062 .H44 2023 (print) | LCC LB1062 (ebook) | DDC 370.15/23—dc23/eng/20220908
LC record available at https://lccn.loc.gov/2022039692
LC ebook record available at https://lccn.loc.gov/2022039693

32 31 30 29 28 27 26 25 24   3 4 5 6 7 8 9 10 11 12

RIGOR BY DESIGN NOT CHANCE

Deeper Thinking Through Actionable Instruction and Assessment

Foreword

Great learning is like great love—of relationships, sports, music, and food. We return to our best friends, favorite teams, and musical artists who jibe with our passions and interests. And just like those experiences, every time we go back to significant learning, we glean a new understanding, insight, or perspective, making learning both additive and generative. This is one of the most important contributions that Karin Hess makes in *Rigor by Design, Not Chance.*

Hess invites us to think about instructional planning as a journey that enables students to experience *far transfer*. And wouldn't it be wonderful if every time we learned something new, it felt like an invitation? It would not be information we *must* learn for compliance or tests, but an offer to take part in an experience that includes choice in a partnership between teachers and students.

This book provides a concrete roadmap for intentional planning for instruction that is student centered; if well implemented, this approach will help learners retain information for a lifetime. We all eventually realize that the memories that stay with us are connected to something personally relevant; the rest we forget because the lack of anchors for new information means it's not encoded in long-term memory. Hess emphasizes how the brain functions as it seeks patterns and makes connections to deeper learning. Thus, explicit instruction is not just planning from a textbook, but also requires building scaffolds and schemas for learning. Without scaffolds, without taking those steps that support the process of cognition, students can get lost when content increases in complexity. It's also noteworthy to point out that Hess defines cognition not just in terms of increasing complexity, but also as including affective (social and emotional) engagement.

The Hess Cognitive Rigor Matrices (created in 2009) now provide a standard methodology for increasing complexity in three arenas: standards, instruction, and assessment. Using the intersection of Bloom's cognitive taxonomy and Webb's Depth of Knowledge

Framework, the matrices not only exemplify how to increase cognitive complexity, but also show teachers how to build scaffolds into the learning process. By using the matrices to build scaffolds for instruction and assessment, teachers can help students achieve greater levels of success with new content as they transfer surface knowledge to more complex contexts. And by building schemas—by helping students create mental folders where they can place and retrieve specific content knowledge—teachers help students build file cabinets in their minds.

Hess's model of planning for instruction helps students grow, digest, and retain new knowledge. So often curricula focus on the totality of textbook content rather than on the needs of learners. Although we have become better at the latter over the years, teachers are still conversing around the globe about what page or chapter they have "covered." When we decide that the only information worth teaching is retainable knowledge, however, the path is clearer.

Hess makes this case while providing a treasure trove of resources and instructional strategies throughout this book. Chapters 2–7 provide multiple strategies to use in lesson planning that convey the purpose and intended outcome of the lesson. With this information in hand, students will be able to replicate these structures later in life.

Hess also advises us to engage students in self-assessment and self-reflection. Just as teachers create plans before, during, and after instructional processes, Hess suggests building in metacognition at each step of the learning. This is probably the most innovative part of this book. Although teaching for metacognition is not a new tenet of learning, building it into the lesson cycle certainly is. When students own their learning—when they understand the instructional strategies, how to back up and move forward in cognition, and when to use prior knowledge as an anchor—they become autonomous learners. This is the basis for equitable instruction; it clarifies the difference between differentiation and scaffolding and between solid Tier 1 instruction and intervention.

Hess also asserts that by first prioritizing learning goals and then building success criteria for learning outcomes, teachers may lead students to deeper learning by focusing on the highest priorities for instruction and assessment. To this end, she synthesizes work by Wiggins and McTighe on backward design and authentic learning tasks.

Hess is an assessment specialist. Although she clarifies the qualities of authentic performance assessments, she also promotes the use of short-cycle formative assessments within simple or complex performance tasks. This is the only way teachers can see where students are in their learning; these data are therefore crucial in knowing how to monitor and adjust instruction daily.

Rigor by Design, Not Chance challenges the very nature of school itself while emphasizing the most salient points of college and career readiness. This work reframes our thoughts on how to provide deeper, more meaningful learning for all students in an equitable manner, and it brings engagement into greater focus as a means of achieving the highest potential for student success.

—Brandon Doubek, EdD, author and chief executive officer, Evolution Alliance, LLC

Acknowledgments

For me, writing a book is truly a collaborative effort, even when my name is the only name on the cover. I'd like to acknowledge the people who became my "thought partners," collectively contributing to the ideas that came together in this book.

First, I'd like to express sincere gratitude to my esteemed colleagues who took time to review early drafts of the manuscript and provide both encouragement and substantive feedback. In the end, their insights and deep knowledge of curriculum, lesson design, and, most important, the diverse learning needs of students resulted in what I hope is a book filled with practical strategies that teachers at any grade level will find fresh and useful.

- Laura Lynn Benson, director of curriculum and professional development for International Schools Services, Princeton, NJ
- Barbara Blackburn, author, Asheville, NC
- Barbara Ewing Cockroft, State Support Team Region 9, Ohio Department of Education, Canton, OH
- Mariane Gfroerer, director of innovation and NHLI/Southern NH University Graduate Program, Hampton, NH
- Ellen Hume-Howard, executive director, New Hampshire Learning Initiative/NHLI, Kingston, NH
- Felicia Sullivan, director of research and evaluation, Jobs for the Future, Lowell, MA
- Jonathan Vander Els, director of collaborative learning, New Hampshire Learning Initiative, Hampton Falls, NH
- Kathy White, director of innovative projects, New Hampshire Learning Initiative, Nashua, NH
- Lynn Shafer Willner, researcher, WIDA at the Wisconsin Center for Education Research, University of Wisconsin-Madison, Manlius, NY

I'd also like to thank several amazing school leaders willing to take a leap of faith and support their teachers over several school years in piloting and giving me feedback on many of the strategies and tools in the book. These dedicated professionals were willing to stay the course and discover with me how to make learning deep and meaningful for every student.

- Yvonne Aguilera, director of learning, leading, and innovation, Midland Independent School District, Midland, TX
- Tanya Bates Howell, founding principal, and Maria Psimadas, assistant principal, PS 349, Magnet School for Leadership and Innovation Through STEAM, New York, NY
- Chris Dodge, director, Salem Career and Technical Education Center, Salem, NH
- Siri Reynolds, principal, Stone Creek Charter School, Edwards, CO
- Steve Rothenberg, director, Concord Regional Technical Center, Concord, NH
- Damarr Smith, senior program manager, competency-based education, Chicago Public Schools, Chicago, IL

Finally, I would like to express gratitude to the staff at ASCD with whom I've worked most closely. In November 2020, senior acquisitions editor Susan Hills contacted me to discuss book ideas and believed in my vision for this book, helping me to organize my thinking around the five major themes. Senior editor Mary Beth Nielsen, working with copyeditor Amy Azzam and art director Donald Ely, then guided me through the editing, design, and production processes to help make the book meaningful and relevant for classroom teachers. Working behind the scenes, they were always responsive to my questions and supportive in representing the essence and intent of my work.

Introduction

Now, more than at any other time in education, teachers have had to rethink not only what is most important to teach and assess, but also what to let go of when challenged by limited instructional time—all while ensuring all students' equitable access to instruction. Also, as a result of the COVID-19 disruptions, they have had to transform their delivery of instruction to maximize student engagement while meeting a variety of needs in face-to-face, remote, and hybrid classrooms.

The good news is that educators—including consultants like me—have had to investigate more effective ways to engage with students to make learning both equitable and personally meaningful. The bad news is that rigor has sometimes suffered in the process in the form of lowered expectations for all or some students. Many of the successful blended learning strategies that came about as a result of the pandemic will continue to be part of school as we now know it. But I hope we don't lose sight of the goal—for each student to achieve deeper learning—as we reimagine more equitable classrooms of the future.

Elsewhere (Hess, 2018a), I have identified three guiding principles for creating learning and assessment tasks that support deeper learning:

- **Deep learning is an essential goal for each student.** We see deep learning when students begin as novices, develop expertise over time, and are able to transfer knowledge and skills to new learning situations in each content area. For example, they might move from formulaic writing to seeing themselves as authors or from following teacher-designed investigations to designing investigations that answer their own curious questions. Deeper learning goes beyond acquiring and applying facts, concepts, and skills. It requires students to know themselves better as learners; they begin to see themselves as problem solvers and as critical, creative thinkers. Students accelerate the learning progress and boost their motivation when they understand the expectations for learning (success criteria); know what they must do to meet a

1

learning target (goal setting and planning); and can self-assess, track progress, and reflect on their own learning.

- **Assessment quality matters.** High-quality assessments—whether formative, interim, or summative—are clearly aligned to rigorous expectations for learning. Teachers design them to be "actionable" in the sense that they uncover both what students know and what still confuses them so that everyone better understands what actions will move learning forward.

- **Learning is at the heart of assessment design and system coherence.** When teachers design assessments to uncover student thinking—not merely what students may have memorized—they can interpret the evidence in student work products to answer the question, *What's next or where to next for this student?* Educators need to understand how the brain processes information during learning and how learning typically develops over time to determine the next optimal steps for learning. This is different from following a prescribed teacher-driven scope and sequence or curriculum guide.

The goal of this book is to provide teachers with practical ways to deepen student engagement, promote a growth mindset, and, ultimately, give students more ownership of their learning. Five essential, evidence-based teacher moves work in conjunction with one another to build a supportive classroom culture for thinking and learning. An easy way to remember them is to use the ABCs:

1. **A**sk a series of probing questions of increasing complexity.
2. **B**uild schemas in each content area.
3. **C**onsider ways to strategically scaffold learning.
4. **D**esign complex tasks that emphasize transfer and evidence-based solutions.
5. **E**ngage students in metacognition and reflection throughout the learning process.

Surely, some readers may be thinking that they already use some or all of these teacher moves. However, implementing them in the way I describe will maximize their effect on student learning and promote deeper engagement.

Why Ask a Series of Probing Questions of Increasing Complexity?

Asking a series of probing questions that increase in depth and complexity is different from asking a single question for students to answer. This approach provides multiple entry points for students to make personal connections with what they already know; it also models for students how they can delve deeper by asking and answering their own questions.

For example, I might begin a math lesson for younger students by showing them photos of two different piles of coins and asking them which group of coins they would rather have. Students have a choice, and there isn't just one correct answer. I want to know more than what they chose. I want to know *why* they chose pile A over pile B and *what thinking they used* to make that determination. (I recall that when my grandson, Tristan, was 4 years old, he told me he didn't want any quarters because they took up too much room in his bank. So he kept the smaller dimes, nickels, and pennies and gave away the quarters so that he could fit in more coins.) After hearing students share their reasoning concerning which pile they chose, I might ask them if they wanted to change their minds based on what they heard, or I might ask pairs of students to make a number sentence or story problem using the coins in the photos.

Instead of focusing on one higher-order question for a lesson, asking a series of open-ended probing questions layers the learning for all students to gradually dig in deeper as they construct meaning for themselves. This approach helps them solidify today's learning and makes it stick beyond tomorrow because students use their own questions to drive the learning.

Why Build Schemas in Each Content Domain?

Mental schemas—also called *mind maps*—are essential to learning because they lay a conceptual foundation for connecting new content and skills with prior learning and experience. Unlike simply reconstructing a concept map provided by the teacher, creating personalized mental maps activates several different areas of the brain, thus building on prior knowledge and simultaneously storing information in many different areas for later retrieval or refinement (Byrne, 2021).

Every content domain has its own schema, meaning the way a given discipline organizes information. Mental schemas help students better understand how the "parts" of a discipline interact to create the whole. For example, these might include analyzing or composing the parts of an essay or a musical piece, designing a mathematical model, or detecting potential design flaws in a science investigation. Building on and using domain-specific schemas to deepen and expand understanding over time are at the heart of all critical and creative thinking.

Why Consider Ways to Strategically Scaffold Learning?

Although most teachers use scaffolding as part of the instructional process, the chosen strategy doesn't always match the intended learning target or support the learning needs of particular students. When engaging students with complex tasks or open-ended problems to solve, considering how and why to use scaffolding will aid in promoting high levels of engagement, and therefore learning.

For example, do students need a complex task broken into smaller steps with frequent checkpoints to support their executive functioning? Or do they need strategies that will help them build language and communication skills? For students who do not need such supports, what are the best ways to strategically move them from foundational to conceptual understanding and then to deeper strategic thinking, planning, and product design? All students can benefit from scaffolding when the purpose matches the demands of the task and supports students' specific learning needs.

Why Design Complex Tasks for All Students?

Complex tasks pose open-ended challenges and provide opportunities for students to decide which tools and processes to use to solve a problem; how they will transfer and demonstrate learning; and how they will support the solutions or connections they've made, from citing sources to analyzing the relevance and accuracy of evidence. Taking on complex tasks prepares students for the authentic problems they will surely face in the real world throughout their lives. When students learn to set goals, struggle productively to find solutions, and learn from earlier mistakes while solving complex problems, they build on their collaboration and self-direction skills.

A high-quality complex task can incorporate all five teacher moves. For example, teachers can begin with a driving question; frame activities to build conceptual schemas; scaffold to support diverse learning needs; build in differentiation by offering choices of content, processes, or products; and ask students to reflect not only on what content they've learned, but also on what they've learned about themselves as learners.

Why Engage Students in Metacognition and Reflection Throughout the Learning Process?

Many teachers use exit cards at the end of a lesson to help students recall something they were just taught. However, the human brain needs time *throughout* the learning cycle to solidify new learning by connecting it to prior, stored learning and then finding a way to make the new information personally relevant (Hess, 2018a). Because the teacher embeds metacognitive strategies in instruction, these strategies don't take time away from teaching.

For example, student-guided instruction should include a self-monitoring process and discussions with peers at certain points during a lesson. Stopping every 10–15 minutes during a lesson to let pairs of students use a turn-and-talk frame with a probing question or conference with a peer is an effective metacognitive strategy that addresses learning *while it is happening*. The other side of the same coin is reflection. Students might reflect on what they have learned in the past that could be useful in solving a new problem or think back on a completed task to figure out how the decisions they made during the problem-solving process led to a new insight or deeper understanding.

Assignments requiring self-reflection and peer-critique activities are also effective ways to encourage reflection on learning *after it has happened*. For example, after completing a task, students might reflect on and evaluate how effectively their group supported group members and worked through conflicts. Engaging students in metacognition and self-reflection before, during, and after each learning opportunity is essential in supporting all students in becoming independent learners.

How the Book Is Organized

Chapter 1 lays a research-based foundation for understanding the meaning of "rigor by design." The following questions frame this first chapter:

- What is deeper learning?
- Why does every student need access to learning that is deep and rigorous?
- How are mental schemas, productive struggle, and neuroscience related?
- What is the connection between cognitive rigor and depth of knowledge?
- How can depth-of-knowledge levels shift teacher–student roles during learning?
- How do the five essential teacher moves work together to create an Actionable Assessment Cycle?

Chapters 2–6 unpack the five essential teacher moves. They define and describe the underlying research that serves as a rationale for using the moves. They offer a variety of teacher-tested strategies to support implementation for both in-person and virtual learning environments. And they conclude with observable student "look for" behaviors that show the move is working.

Chapter 7 provides three views of rigor-by-design implementation. **The student's perspective** refers to rigorous expectations that support students in driving their own learning. **The teacher's perspective** looks at how lesson planning and assessment planning incorporate the five essential teacher moves to build coherence and rigor across the school year. And **the system perspective** refers to teacher-friendly supports that school leaders and instructional coaches can offer when observing in classrooms as they assess teacher questioning strategies, the quality of classroom discourse, the levels of cognitive engagement, and the teacher's actionable uses of assessment.

Teachers need to think of themselves as coaches, guiding students to build a solid foundation, raise their own questions, work more independently, and develop more authentic products to demonstrate their learning. In the end, it's all about students owning and driving their learning.

1

Rigor by Design: Laying the Foundation for Deeper Learning

We live in a fast-changing world. Every two years, the amount of digital information more than doubles. What is novel today may become quickly outdated. Experts predict that nearly two-thirds of elementary school students will one day hold a job that hasn't been created yet. But our schools look the same as they did in the industrial era. The United States used to lead the world in education. Now, other countries are better at preparing their students for the 21st century, while our schools lag behind. Deeper learning calls for a better education so that our students build skills that will help them succeed in school and get the jobs of tomorrow.

—Neha Singh Gohil, "Why Is Deeper Learning Important?"

Today, we expect all students to be ready for the challenges of the 21st century—to learn more, master new technologies, and apply their learning in real-world contexts. The phrase *deeper learning* has generated varied descriptions of the skills, knowledge, and dispositions students must possess to sit at the table of opportunity and succeed in 21st century life and careers.

What Is Deeper Learning?

The most succinct description of deeper learning that I've come across is outlined in the Deeper Learning Framework from the Hewlett Foundation (2013, pp. 2–5). This framework identifies six broad competencies essential to preparing students to achieve at high levels—competencies you can actualize when you purposefully implement the five essential teacher moves. The competencies are as follows:

- **Mastering core academic content** builds a foundation of procedural knowledge and conceptual understanding in each content discipline that students can draw from and transfer to new learning situations.

- **Thinking critically and solving complex problems** go beyond core content, requiring students to formulate questions to investigate, use reasoning and analysis skills, and explore problems and solutions from multiple perspectives.

- **Working collaboratively on complex tasks** builds both personal and workplace skills; students learn to equitably consider multiple points of view, develop problem-solving steps to accomplish tasks, and monitor progress on shared goals.

- **Communicating effectively** begins with learning how to use the terminology, tools, and schemas of each content discipline to organize information in meaningful ways, give and receive feedback to clarify or elaborate on complex ideas or solutions, and demonstrate understanding by tailoring a message to the intended audience, including oneself, peers, adults, or the broader community.

- **Learning how to learn** requires shifting the traditional roles of teachers and students so that students take increased ownership in monitoring their progress on personal goals for learning, seeking resources and help when needed, and reflecting on how strategies they have used and decisions they have made have affected their learning.

- **Developing an academic mindset** leads to positive attitudes and beliefs about oneself as a learner, influencing a student's level of engagement with learning and desire to actively learn from and with others. Academic mindsets build a strong sense of belonging within the learning community because each student is willing to put forth effort, take risks, and persevere when confronted with complex tasks.

Deeper learning is only possible when students become actively immersed in challenging tasks that require them to seek out and acquire new knowledge, apply what they have learned, and build on that learning to construct new knowledge. *This will not happen in classrooms where compliance is the norm.* If we expect students to be curious and think deeply, we need to create a classroom culture where *thinking* is the norm. Do we value—and model—open-ended questions that have more than one answer? Do we value—and honor—learning from mistakes? Are we willing to shift some of our control to students so that they can begin to own their learning?

Understanding the interconnections among these six deeper learning competencies is a good starting point for developing a shared vision within your school of what deeper learning can look like and for planning steps to implement practices that lead to deeper learning. I call this *rigor by design, not chance.*

Why Deep Learning?

College- and career-readiness (CCR) standards establish expectations for all students to demonstrate learning through the acquisition of content knowledge and skills—*and* to be able to transfer that learning to new and more complex tasks over time. The content standards, however, provide little or no guidance to educators as to how, when, or to what degree they should emphasize specific skills and concepts to achieve deeper learning. Without a clear, shared vision of what makes learning deep and rigorous, and without systematically applying that vision to engage students of all ages in rich learning tasks, schools will fail to teach and assess many important college- and career-readiness skills and dispositions, resulting in inequitable learning opportunities for many students. Some students will leave school unprepared for continuing their education or career training.

Research identifies both academic and personal skills and dispositions that students need to be successful in life after high school, no matter what career path they choose. Hess and colleagues (2014) describe three essential CCR skill sets that will help students become self-directed, autonomous learners in any content area (see Figure 1.1). However, implementing these requires educators to dramatically shift the roles of students and teachers throughout the learning process.

Each of the three CCR skill sets addresses unique strategies for deepening learning. Let's look at each of them.

CCR Skill Set 1. Integrating Academics and Crosscutting Skills in Cognitively Demanding Learning Tasks

Two essential teacher moves support this CCR skill set: building schemas in each content domain and designing complex tasks. Students using this skill set successfully engage with tasks that apply deeper learning competencies by mastering core content, thinking critically and solving complex problems, and communicating their understanding with precision and accuracy.

This skill set gives students multiple opportunities to tackle cognitively demanding tasks in every content area using the key cognitive processes of precision of thought, critical thinking, and abstract reasoning. These skills must interact within the context of a specific content domain. Teaching or assessing skills in isolation or applying them within simplistic contexts (for example, offering routine math word problems in place of more complex problem solving) falls short of the goal of deeper learning.

FIGURE 1.1
Three Interrelated College- and Career-Readiness (CCR) Skill Sets

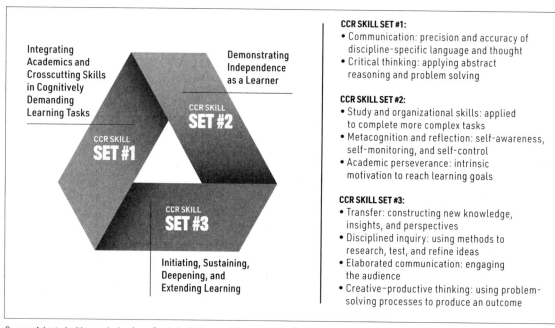

Integrating Academics and Crosscutting Skills in Cognitively Demanding Learning Tasks

Demonstrating Independence as a Learner

CCR SKILL **SET #1**

CCR SKILL **SET #2**

CCR SKILL **SET #3**

Initiating, Sustaining, Deepening, and Extending Learning

CCR SKILL SET #1:
- Communication: precision and accuracy of discipline-specific language and thought
- Critical thinking: applying abstract reasoning and problem solving

CCR SKILL SET #2:
- Study and organizational skills: applied to complete more complex tasks
- Metacognition and reflection: self-awareness, self-monitoring, and self-control
- Academic perseverance: intrinsic motivation to reach learning goals

CCR SKILL SET #3:
- Transfer: constructing new knowledge, insights, and perspectives
- Disciplined inquiry: using methods to research, test, and refine ideas
- Elaborated communication: engaging the audience
- Creative-productive thinking: using problem-solving processes to produce an outcome

Source: Adapted with permission from *Ready for College and Career? Achieving the Common Core Standards and Beyond Through Deeper, Student-Centered Learning* (p. 11), by K. Hess, B. Gong, and R. Steinitz, 2014, Nellie Mae Education Foundation.

Using rich performance tasks and engaging in Socratic seminars are excellent means of integrating these cognitive processes in meaningful, student-centered ways. When integrated with specific academic content, these skills yield more challenging—and ideally, more engaging—learning activities for students (Paige et al., 2013).

Evidence suggests that when classrooms foster precision of thought, critical thinking, and the application of abstract reasoning and challenge students to solve new or nonroutine problems, students begin to build expertise in the discipline-specific knowledge and dispositions they will need in college and future careers (Hess et al., 2014). They learn to reason like a mathematician; investigate like a scientist; and read and write like a historian, technician, or literary critic. When curriculum developers and educators systematically base classroom discourse, instruction, and assessment tasks on these skills, they take a crucial first step toward preparing students for the challenges of postsecondary learning.

Remember, what educators focus on sends a strong signal to students about what is important for them to learn. When *authentic tasks* play a key role in teaching and assessing, such as creating an awareness campaign, a business plan, a how-to tutorial, or an infographic, students will know that teachers expect them to apply their knowledge in ways the world values outside of school.

CCR Skill Set 2. Demonstrating Independence as a Learner

Three essential teacher moves support this skill set: designing complex tasks, strategically scaffolding learning, and engaging students in metacognition. Students developing independence as learners apply several deeper learning competencies: They learn how to learn, how to effectively communicate, and how to develop an academic mindset.

For students to successfully engage with complex, multistep tasks, they also need to develop the personal skills of self-direction and independence. Study and organizational skills help students manage time and sustain the effort needed to learn complex content. Teachers can embed these skills in curricular projects and performance-based tasks. Metacognitive skills are more abstract than organizational skills but are equally important. Students with a grasp of metacognition can reflect on their own learning, develop positive identities as learners, and frame the direction of their own learning and career goals. Because traditional curricula do not typically include metacognitive activities, many students do not learn how to capitalize on their learning or develop self-efficacy (Savitz-Romer & Bouffard, 2012). Educators can foster metacognitive skills through carefully planned activities, such as having students engage in self-reflective tasks; manage their own personal learning portfolios; and conference with adults, peers, and outside mentors.

The most abstract intrapersonal disposition in this skill set is academic perseverance. Although some researchers caution that more research is needed to determine the causal relationship between perseverance and performance (Farrington et al., 2012), some studies suggest that perseverance and a passion for long-term goals may be better predictors of college and career success than either IQ or test scores (Duckworth et al., 2007). People with academic perseverance work strenuously toward challenges, maintaining effort and interest over time, even in the face of adversity. Vague extrinsic goals, such as getting a good grade or a college degree, can rarely sustain learners in the long run. Perseverance depends on intrinsic motivation, which gives individuals the patience and stamina to reach personal long-term goals (Duckworth et al., 2007).

We can't teach self-efficacy, academic perseverance, and intrinsic motivation, but we can develop and nurture them through concrete strategies that emphasize the real-world relevance of academic content, that provide effort-oriented feedback, and that encourage students to develop meaningful rationales for their long-term goals. As Farrington and colleagues (2012) noted, although some students are more likely to persist in tasks or exhibit self-discipline than others, all students are more likely to demonstrate perseverance if the school or classroom context helps them develop positive mindsets and effective learning strategies. Teachers can accomplish this by developing students' academic mindsets and metacognitive and self-regulatory skills, rather than trying to change their innate tendency to persevere.

CCR Skill Set 3. Initiating, Sustaining, Deepening, and Extending Learning

All five essential teacher moves support this skill set, which prepares students for deeper self-directed learning. This skill set develops when teachers and curricula routinely expect students to extend prior content learning; think flexibly; and apply their cognitive skills of interpreting, evaluating, and synthesizing to produce deeper understanding and initiate and solve authentic complex problems, such as independent investigations and case study analyses. Newmann and colleagues (2007) call this learning *authentic intellectual work*. Its key components include the construction of knowledge, the use of disciplined inquiry (appropriate to the given content domain), and the creation of products that have value beyond school. Contrasted with memorizing information and using routine procedures, the construction of knowledge involves building on prior knowledge to investigate novel problems and complex ideas. As students clarify or elaborate on ideas or information, they learn how to communicate in more sophisticated ways, using appropriate verbal, symbolic, and visual strategies for presenting the results of their work.

Creative–productive thinking is another key element of this skill set. In a seminal paper, Perkins (1984) emphasized the relationship between creativity and productivity:

> Creative thinking is thinking patterned in a way that leads to creative results....The ultimate criterion for creativity is output. We call a person creative when that person consistently gets creative results, meaning, roughly speaking, original and otherwise appropriate results by the criteria of the domain in question. (pp. 18–19)

Productive thinking often involves a tension between evaluative critical thinking and creative innovation. Viewing a situation or topic from new perspectives increases creativity, sparking creative–productive thinking. This kind of thinking not only encourages risk-taking and flexible thinking behaviors, but it also expands the ability to construct—rather than just reproduce—knowledge. Students typically won't develop these skills by chance; it requires implementing strategies that encourage choice, decision making, and student-designed tasks (such as choice boards, menus, playlists, and stations). Curricula should build in time for this work. Research (Newmann et al., 2007) has shown that across content areas and regardless of race, gender, or socioeconomic status, students in grades 3–12 who experienced instruction that promoted these skills demonstrated higher achievement overall than students who experienced more traditional curricular approaches.

Mental Schemas, Productive Struggle, and Neuroscience

For almost two decades, my work has focused on researching deeper learning, developing strategies that support rigorous and accessible instruction, and developing assessment designs that uncover thinking. Drawing from cognitive sciences research (Brown et al., 2014; Oakley et al., 2021; Sousa, 2015, 2022; Willis, 2021), we know that one crucial aspect of cognitive engagement is the ability to make connections, rather than simply memorizing and practicing the retrieval of facts and performing routine procedures in isolation. Connecting new information to prior learning and real-world contexts helps students both consolidate new learning and build mental schemas. Schemas are cognitive frameworks that organize and interpret relevant information, such as knowing which characteristics distinguish a literary text from an informational or argument-based text (Hess, 2018a).

Making connections throughout the learning process develops long-term memory storage and strengthens mental pathways as brain signals travel from neuron to neuron. The retrieval of related information and the storage of new information become more fluid and flexible over time. But making connections is only the first step to deeper learning. Engaging in productive struggle with challenging tasks (Sriram, 2020) further spurs the production of myelin, a substance that increases the strength of brain signals. Designing lessons that build schemas, that create opportunities for productive struggle, and that require students to transfer their skills and knowledge to new situations is what truly makes learning—and instruction—rigorous by design.

The Brain and Deeper Learning: A "Handy" Model

An easy way to illustrate how the brain looks and acts during learning is through this updated version of a multisensory activity I used with my own students (Hess, 1985). Doing this short activity right now will actually help you visualize how the brain works and remember this information.

The Corpus Callosum and the Two Hemispheres of the Brain

Make two fists and place them together with fingernails touching. Your curled fingers represent about 5/6 of your total brain's size. Your arms are the "information highway" (*spinal cord*) that connects the body's *nervous system* to the brain and coordinates simple reflexes, such as automatically sending a signal to instantly pull your hand away from a hot object.

Your fingernails represent the *corpus callosum*, physically separating the two hemispheres of the brain and allowing communication back and forth. In almost all mammals, the brain hemispheres function independently of one another. This means that at any given time, the left or the right hemisphere is in control of your mental processing and physical activity, so you need to practice "switching" back and forth, fluidly using both sides of your brain during learning. For example, memorizing how to spell or define a word would be stored in the left hemisphere, whereas visual metaphors and experiences illustrating the word's meanings would be stored holistically in the right side. Long-term retention is stronger when learning activities use both hemispheres to connect words, symbols, text, or concepts with sensory images and experiences.

For native speakers of English, the left hemisphere is often associated with understanding and using logic and language, whereas the right side is more visually oriented, involved in activities such as visual imagery and face recognition. The right side of the brain tends to process information as a whole, rather than as individual details. It also tends to process information more intuitively or randomly, such as when a learner is letting the mind wander when daydreaming, listening to music, or "messing around" with manipulatives. When the brain switches from *focused mode* to *diffuse mode*, working memory gets out of the way and random connections help students grapple mentally with tough ideas (Oakley et al., 2021). As a matter of fact, learners must allow their brains to move back and forth between focused and diffuse modes when applying creative thinking processes and generating and testing possible solutions. The right side of the brain is also thought to be involved in spatial abilities, such as when you judge the position of things in space or when athletes determine their body position in relation to other players in a game.

Four Brain Lobes and Their Functions

With your fists still closed, now look at your pinky fingers. These represent the vision center (*occipital lobe*) at the base of the brain in the back of your head. This explains why you black out or get dizzy and "see stars" if you get hit there. Now move to your ring fingers. These represent the *temporal lobe* (just above your occipital lobe), where sensory input (visual, auditory, tactile, olfactory) is processed through communication with the hippocampus, leading to the retention of visual memories, language recognition, and emotional associations. When a situation such as being afraid to talk in front of a group is stored as a stressful memory, the negative emotions associated with that memory often diminish or block retention. Conversely, enjoying acting out a story while hearing it read aloud can aid in the retention and retrieval of story details.

Your middle fingers (above your temporal lobe) represent the *parietal lobe*. The parietal lobe integrates sensory information (such as touching, tasting, and smelling) from various parts of the body with motor skills that control body movements (arms, hands, eye movements, and so on) so that you can open a door, draw a picture, or throw a ball. When you touch items and count them out loud, you're using the parietal lobe.

Your occipital, temporal, and parietal lobes are hard at work when you're building basic skills and a conceptual foundation, whether you're acquiring language skills for reading, writing, and speaking or learning how to perform routine mathematics and science procedures. But you can't solve complex problems, think critically and abstractly, or develop creative products without engaging your frontal lobe.

The pointer fingers and thumbs toward the front of your fists represent the largest area of the brain behind your forehead, called the *frontal lobe* or *neocortex*. This is where reasoning, problem solving, working through productive struggles, controlling impulses, and making decisions and ethical judgments take place. The prefrontal cortex, part of the frontal lobe, is responsible for the brain's executive function, acting like a conductor communicating, guiding, and coordinating messages from the other lobes of the brain. This region of the brain is unique to humans, regulating both short-term or working memory and long-term decision making, enabling us to plan ahead, develop strategies, and adjust actions or reactions in changing situations. In addition, it helps us focus thoughts, pay attention, and concentrate on goals, and it enables us to consider several different yet related lines of thinking when learning or evaluating complex concepts or tasks. This includes mediating conflicting thoughts, making choices, and predicting the probable outcomes of actions or events. This brain area is most strongly implicated in human qualities like consciousness, general intelligence, and personality.

The ability to project future consequences resulting from current actions, make choices between good and bad actions (or better and best), and override and suppress socially unacceptable responses is processed in the *neocortex*. This is the last part of the brain to develop as we acquire understandings of global unity and higher forms of love, empathy, friendship, and beauty. It takes about 25 years for this region of the brain to fully mature. Can you think of examples of when teenagers or young adults have made poor decisions based solely on emotions or done some really dumb and dangerous things? That's often the result of a not yet fully developed neocortex.

Learning the importance of sharing and teamwork or getting involved with community service projects uses the frontal lobe to build the sense of empathy and friendship. Analyzing flawed characters in stories and history or debating current issues that present moral dilemmas are also ways to practice using the frontal lobe.

The Limbic System: Motivation, Attention, and Retention

Thinking that leads to deeper cognitive engagement starts with emotional engagement. And "as it turns out, engagement follows a hierarchy: emotional, cognitive, and then behavioral" (Almarode, 2018, p. 2). Because assessments measure observable skills, thoughts, and dispositions, teachers must first attend to emotional engagement during learning. And that takes us to the limbic system, in the midbrain.

Separate and open your fists to look at your palms. There you'll find the *limbic system*. Connections between your stored memories and your emotions begin here. The limbic system is responsible for your emotional expressions (such as laughing or grimacing) and interactions that enhance or inhibit engagement, deep learning, and memory.

Two large limbic system structures, the *amygdala* and *hippocampus* (located in the temporal lobe), play important roles in memory storage. The amygdala determines which memories are stored and where based on how much an event can invoke an emotional response, whether positive or negative. The hippocampus sends memories to the appropriate part of the cerebral hemisphere for long-term storage and retrieves them when needed. Damage to this area of the brain may result in an inability to form new memories.

Think about how an enjoyable learning activity engages you (and your brain) and is easy to remember afterward, whereas a scary past event (such as taking a test) can make your brain shut down and send you into survival mode. Learning situations perceived as pleasant or painful will result in the body producing endorphins. Endorphins can inhibit the pain signals or produce a feeling of euphoria, often compared to a "runner's high." How you react emotionally while learning really *does* make a difference in your level of engagement and in how much you actually learn and are able to remember.

When you understand how emotions affect levels of engagement, motivation, and deeper cognitive processing, it's easy to conclude that all learning—especially social and emotional learning—begins in the limbic system. This mindset should be at the heart of all instructional planning.

Seven Misconceptions About Rigor and Depth of Knowledge

Some educators misinterpret cognitive rigor to simply mean asking students to do more work, understand "harder" or more abstract content, or complete complex tasks independently. This instructional approach to rigor can create inequity in what we expect of different students and, ultimately, in how we teach them.

Before we can design rigorous instruction, let's dispel some common misconceptions about rigor and depth of knowledge (Hess, 2018a, 2018b).

Misconception 1. All students can't think deeply; all students shouldn't need scaffolding to support deeper thinking.

When high-performing adults take on complex challenges, they benefit from supports, such as chunking texts, using exemplar models, and working with peers. The same is true for students. All students *can* think deeply; it's up to us to find ways to scaffold learning so that students can move from acquiring foundational skills to engaging in the deeper thinking that happens in the frontal lobe of the brain. Consider the thinking behind Vygotsky's zone of proximal development (1978): When a challenge is just beyond a student's current level of independent mastery, social interaction and discourse can bridge gaps in understanding, so learning moves forward. Working on complex tasks with others lays the foundation for independently producing high-quality products in the future. Collaboration and discourse are not cheating; they are some of the best ways for students to learn how to express and support their reasoning.

Misconception 2. Depth-of-knowledge levels should function as a taxonomy.

Many educators are familiar with two models describing levels of thinking. Bloom's taxonomy (Bloom et al., 1956) was originally developed to describe test questions on college exams. Both the original version and the revised Bloom's taxonomy (Anderson et al., 2001) were conceived as a hierarchy describing lower to higher levels of thinking, where "lower-order" thinking (remembering, understanding, and applying) is devalued in favor of analyzing, evaluating, and creating.

Norman Webb (1997) developed his Depth of Knowledge (DOK) Framework to describe curricular expectations. Alignment studies used the framework to examine how closely test questions on state assessments matched the state's content standards. The DOK framework comprises four levels:

- **DOK level 1. Recall and reproduction.** This level requires students to retrieve memorized facts and use routine procedures (for example, identify who/what/where, calculate, apply formulas, use reference materials).
- **DOK level 2. Basic skills and concepts.** This level requires some mental processing and decision making beyond simply recalling or reproducing a response (for example, summarize, sequence, compare and contrast, predict, make observations).
- **DOK level 3. Strategic thinking and reasoning.** At this level, students go beyond a basic comprehension of a text or an explanation of a concept to answer open-ended questions requiring reasoning, planning, and supporting evidence (for example, analyze a viewpoint, draw conclusions from a science investigation, solve a novel real-world problem).
- **DOK level 4. Extended thinking.** This level requires engaging in complex reasoning, planning, and using supporting evidence from multiple sources (for example, critique the effect of a given event on history, develop complex multimedia products). Tasks at this level usually take more time to complete, although time is not a deciding factor in determining whether an assignment is at DOK 4.

If DOK levels had been developed as a taxonomy, the assumption would be that extended thinking (DOK 4) is better than strategic thinking (DOK 3), which is better than conceptual understanding (DOK 2), which is better than recall of foundational knowledge (DOK 1). Taxonomies tend to devalue the role of foundational skills and conceptual understanding in laying the groundwork for deeper thinking and understanding. In reality, DOK 1 activities (such as acquiring vocabulary and learning routine skills and procedures) and DOK 2 tasks (such as identifying the main idea, organizing data, and solving word problems) prepare students for solving more complex, nonroutine mathematics problems requiring reasoning and proof or for analyzing complex texts. In reality, DOK levels do *not* represent a taxonomy; they describe different and deeper ways to interact with content.

Misconception 3. You can equate verb lists with depth-of-knowledge levels.

Have you seen that visual of a wheel divided into four DOK levels, with verbs in each section? I call this the "DOK Wheel of Misfortune," because it suggests that if you spin the wheel and pick a verb, your students will instantly think deeply. In fact, verbs without content tell you very little about task complexity. Verbs and the DOK wheel imply a connection that really doesn't exist. Let's use the verb *draw* to illustrate this point. "Draw a circle" requires simple recall and is not as complex as "draw a line of best fit on a scatterplot," which requires conceptual understanding and decision making.

Here's what we know about verbs as an indicator of task complexity:

- Verbs describe a *type* of thinking, not the depth of understanding or level of cognitive engagement with content.
- Verbs are generic, void of content. The same verb applies differently in different content areas. Analyzing a literary text requires the use of different schemas and thought processes than analyzing a work of art.
- Some of the same verbs appear at multiple levels of Bloom's taxonomy; using them to determine the level of complexity of a given test item or task is therefore a subjective exercise.
- What comes *after* the verb determines the complexity of an assessment task or a learning activity.

Misconception 4. Depth of knowledge is about greater difficulty, more effort, or learning to do harder things.

Dictionaries define the word *rigor* using synonyms such as *inflexible*, *hard*, *rigid*, and *strict*. But cognitive rigor is just the opposite—it's thinking flexibly and seeing multiple possibilities, approaches, or possible perspectives. Uncovering multiple perspectives or approaches to a problem means understanding concepts deeply and applying them broadly. Debate coaches often require students to prepare for both sides of the debate. Debaters have to be flexible enough to use the evidence on each side to argue for either the claim or counterclaim at a moment's notice. This kind of thinking requires use of the frontal lobe of the brain.

Some tasks are hard to do, but they're not cognitively rigorous. Many things we learn as a beginner (such as skiing or long division) are difficult to do at first, but when we memorize the basics and practice the routines, they become more automatic. Decoding words may be challenging at first, but with practice these tasks become easier. Conversely, learning how to determine an author's purpose, theme, or potential bias requires strategic thinking and decision making.

Misconception 5. You can assess all depth-of-knowledge levels with multiple-choice questions.

This claim doesn't make sense when you consider the level of engagement with content that DOK 3 and DOK 4 tasks require. Constructed-response questions, performance tasks, or extended projects are more suited for teaching and assessing the use of more complex tasks. To be clear, you can assess DOK 3 questions that focus on strategic thinking and reasoning with multiple-choice items. However, when a student selects the "best" option, such as locating supporting text evidence for a stated theme, his or her response—whether correct or incorrect—provides little insight into how that student applied concepts and reasoning to arrive at the answer or whether the response is a result of guessing or, in the case of an absence of response, just inadvertently skipping the item completely. Multiple-choice questions work best for questions having only one correct response: DOK 1 and DOK 2 questions. To better understand student thinking, I suggest identifying a few of the multiple-choice questions you think your students might struggle with and asking them to write a short explanation describing why they chose that answer over the others. Explanations can uncover thinking and misconceptions.

Misconception 6. Higher-order thinking always leads to deeper understanding.

We typically associate the higher levels of Bloom's taxonomy—analyzing, evaluating, and creating—with the phrase *higher-order thinking*. However, many creative activities don't lead to the deeper thinking needed to, say, investigate an essential question. Critical thinking activities begin by building a conceptual foundation (DOK 2) so that students can apply that understanding and transfer learning to new or more complex contexts (DOK 3 or 4). We see, therefore, that all levels of thinking have value; the goal of rigor by design is to be intentional about how to balance those levels throughout an "actionable" learning and assessment cycle.

Misconception 7. Tasks requiring multiple steps, or the use of multiple or complex texts or resources, will lead to deeper thinking.

All multistep tasks are not created equal; many are actually learned routines. These include applying skills and rules that are important to know but are still foundational (DOK 1). Think about long division. It can have many steps and can be hard to do at first, but it's still a routine operation done the same way every time.

Contrast the long division assignment with researching a topic, which also has multiple steps. Students might begin by building foundational knowledge; they might brainstorm what they know about the topic, learn new terms and vocabulary, or conduct a key word search—all DOK 1–type tasks. Then they might make connections among terms and concepts or examine cause and effect relationships and generate questions to investigate (DOK 2). Finally, they might gather data to help answer a broader, issue-based question (DOK 3 or 4). The steps of this process may begin as routine, but later on, they involve planning and strategic thinking. The number of steps is *not* the determining factor of cognitive rigor. What deepens complexity and learning is the nonroutine nature of how one step might lead to any number of decisions regarding other steps in the process. Students achieve deeper understanding when they dive into the concept and come away with new understandings and insights, making connections that can transfer to future learning.

Cognitive Rigor and Engagement

Three factors influence cognitive rigor (Hess et al., 2009). The first is *cognitive engagement with the content*—and that begins with emotional engagement when students make personal connections that answer such questions as, *Why do I want to learn this?* or *How is this relevant to me?* The second factor is *the complexity of the content:* concrete as opposed to abstract, literal as opposed to figurative, or practical as opposed to theoretical. The third factor involves *the scope of the learning activity,* especially when students are called on to analyze or interpret multiple sources of evidence or develop a complex product of learning, such as a research project, podcast, or multimedia presentation.

So which behaviors and skills indicate that students are cognitively engaged? Here are some things to look for.

Students are cognitively engaged when they

- Make and support connections to consolidate their learning.
- Build schemas by taking something apart, naming the parts, and analyzing how—or how effectively—the parts work together.
- Generate open-ended questions that lead to student-driven investigations.
- Define a challenge or problem and plan a solution path.
- Engage with peers through collaboration and discourse that uncovers thinking and reasoning.
- Apply what they have learned to novel situations, also known as *far transfer*.

To make these observable components of cognitive rigor student-friendly, I created rigor-by-design task cards that you can print as a classroom poster or cut apart to use as six individual cards (see "Related Resources" at the end of this chapter). Teachers can use the task cards as metacognitive prompts when students engage in collaborative discourse or work through a complex challenge. Some teachers print and cut the cards apart to create a cube that they can roll like dice to randomly select a prompt for small-group discussion. Prompts include, for example, "build schema" and "generate open-ended questions." I've used a simplified version of the task cards cube with my 1st grade granddaughter, who enjoys playing the "thinking game."

DOK Levels and Shifting Teacher–Student Roles

Teachers take on different roles when planning and delivering instruction. They use directed teaching to help learners acquire new information and basic skills. At times, they will shift to become a facilitator, guiding learners to actively process information or practice a new procedure. When teachers take on the roles of directors and facilitators, students receive and reproduce what the teacher has presented. These teacher roles are most effective when students are acquiring new skills and vocabulary (DOK 1) and developing basic conceptual understanding (DOK 2). However, they are not as effective when we want students to engage in self-direction, collaboration, creative problem solving, and reasoning activities.

A third role is that of strategic coach; here, the teacher becomes an observer, providing resources and a structure for the DOK 3–type tasks that students need to complete, while offering opportunities for student choice and decision making. Just as a coach would do while watching soccer players during a game, teachers who are strategic coaches offer ongoing scaffolding and targeted feedback to support students in improving their performance. Coaching creates a classroom culture of shared responsibility between teachers and students, with teachers giving up some control to students, who engage in student-driven projects and open-ended investigations (DOK 4). Shifting to a coaching role is most successful when students have learned how to collaborate or conduct research before the teacher builds those expectations into a more complex and challenging project requiring those skills. Figure 1.2 provides a general overview of how teacher and student roles shift at each DOK level.

My greatest "aha" moment about the Depth of Knowledge Framework was the realization that when we design with rigor and deeper learning in mind, DOK levels become a subtle but powerful force in shifting from teacher-directed to student-driven learning. *This is the single most important use of the Depth of Knowledge Framework—to guide the design of rigorous, student-directed learning.* At DOK 1 and DOK 2, teachers are directing learning, and students are receiving and recalling information and using *near transfer* (replicating what they were taught). At DOK 3 and DOK 4, teachers are strategically coaching learning, and students are driving the direction of learning. In lesson planning, we need to think more about how to move students from acquiring and replicating foundational information to applying it in novel situations (*far transfer*) using complex DOK 3 and DOK 4 tasks.

One goal of rigor by design is planning lessons that reach DOK 3 thinking, such as asking students to respond to open-ended questions requiring supporting evidence; solve problem-based performance tasks; or reflect on their own learning, citing work samples as evidence. Reaching DOK 4 in every lesson is not possible; however, teachers should allow adequate time in a unit to offer extended-learning activities, such as project-based learning. (For a more in-depth discussion of lesson and unit planning with a range of DOK levels, see Chapter 7.)

A Word About the Hess Cognitive Rigor Matrices

For a more detailed view of how the different DOK levels affect the roles of teachers and students in different subject areas, take a look at the Hess Cognitive Rigor Matrices (CRMs) (see "Related Resources" at the end of this chapter). I initially developed an early prototype of the matrices for language arts/social studies and mathematics/science. I used those matrices with teachers to examine classroom assignments at different grade levels and in different content areas. I found that in many classrooms, teachers were not routinely teaching and assessing the deeper rigor described in the content standards. Most assignments I

FIGURE 1.2
Teacher–Student Roles and Depth-of-Knowledge (DOK) Levels

DOK Levels and Focus	Teacher Roles: Planned Strategies	Student Roles: Observable Evidence of Learning
Level 1. Acquire a foundation.	• Uses questions to focus attention. (*Who? What? Where? How? When?*) • Directs, leads, demonstrates, defines. • Monitors practice. • Scaffolds for access and focus.	• Acquires vocabulary, facts, rules, routines. • Memorizes, recites, quotes, restates. • Retrieves information; uses required tools and resources. • Practices and self-monitors routine skills. • Seeks support; asks questions to clarify procedures or task expectations.
Level 2. Use, connect, and generalize.	• Uses questions to build schemas: differentiate parts from the whole, classify, explain relationships. (*Can you explain examples/ nonexamples? Cause/effect?*) • Draws out basic inferences. • Models or scaffolds conceptual understanding. (*Why? Under what conditions?*) • Provides guided practice for multistep tasks.	• Explains relationships, sorts, classifies, compares, organizes information, summarizes. • Makes predictions based on estimates, observations, prior knowledge. • Proposes problems, topics, or questions to investigate. • Raises conceptual questions. (*Why? What if?*) • Selects tool or strategy for specific purpose. • Follows teacher-designed procedures.
Level 3. Deepen and construct meaning.	• Uses questions to probe reasoning, thinking, planning. (*How will you know or do this? Where is the evidence?*) • Promotes peer discourse and self-reflection to uncover big ideas, themes. • Designs tasks requiring proof, justification, analysis of evidence quality, accuracy. • Models or scaffolds validating sources. • Supports student-designed performance tasks.	• Uncovers relevant, accurate, credible information; flaws in a design; or proposed solutions linked with big ideas, themes. • Raises questions that explore underlying meanings. (*Is that what the author is saying? What can we learn from this?*) • Plans how to develop supporting (hard) evidence for conclusions, solutions, claims. • Researches, tests, and revises ideas; solves nonroutine problems. • Sets goals; monitors progress. • Self-assesses; uses feedback to improve quality.
Level 4. Extend, transfer, and broaden meaning.	• Uses questions to challenge or extend meaning (big ideas, themes); explore sources; broaden perspectives. (*Are there potential biases? Can you propose an alternative model?*) • Models or scaffolds triangulating sources, peer-to-peer critique, self-reflection. • Supports student-designed performance tasks. • Promotes peer discourse and self-reflections to uncover big ideas, themes, trends.	• Initiates, transfers, and constructs new knowledge; links insights to big ideas, themes. • Modifies, creates, elaborates based on analysis and interpretation of multiple sources. • Raises novel questions; investigates real-world problems and issues. • Sets goals; monitors progress. • Self-manages time and tasks. • Generates self-reflections; self-assesses and uses feedback to improve work quality.

Source: From *Linking Research with Practice: A Local Assessment Toolkit to Guide School Leaders* (p. 5), by K. Hess, 2013, Educational Research in Action. Reprinted with permission.

analyzed looked more like sports teams doing practice drills than players transferring those skills to effectively play a game. Analyzing examples of what teachers thought were rigorous assignments led to my next conceptual leap in refining the Hess CRMs. Drawing from cognitive sciences, I began to understand how each content domain had a unique schema.

The updated Hess CRMs show what rigor looks like in eight subject areas: reading and listening, math and science, written and oral communication, social studies and humanities, fine arts, health and physical education, world languages, and career and technical education. Figure 1.3 shows a matrix for reading and listening.

The Importance of Actionable Instruction and Assessment

On any given day in my teaching career, I assessed students by listening, observing, conferencing, designing performance tasks and small-group investigations, giving quizzes and tests, and administering standardized tests required by my school district or state. Because only some of these assessments were useful in advancing the learning of my students, I simply ignored results I couldn't immediately use and moved on. It took me several years to deepen my understanding of what makes an assessment "actionable" and how best to use the results—the most important use being to advance the learning of each individual student.

The Actionable Assessment Cycle

Using assessment evidence to continually advance learning and empower learners requires three actions on the part of teachers:

- The teacher designs assessment questions and tasks to uncover what the student is thinking, not simply what the student remembers.
- The teacher can interpret the assessment evidence in terms of where a student is *right now* along their learning continuum (not necessarily the teacher's teaching continuum).
- The teacher uses assessment evidence to provide actionable feedback to students to help them develop self-reflection skills and better understand themselves as learners, in addition to understanding the content at hand.

The Actionable Assessment Cycle begins with having a series of clear learning targets; engaging students to uncover their thinking related to the learning targets; and eliciting observable, measurable evidence indicating whether they are ready to move on to the next new learning. If you think this sounds a lot like the formative uses of assessment, you're

FIGURE 1.3

Hess Cognitive Rigor Matrix (CRM): Reading and Listening

Integrating Depth-of-Knowledge Levels with Bloom's Cognitive Process Dimensions

Revised Bloom's Taxonomy	DOK 1 Recall and Reproduction	DOK 2 Skills and Concepts	DOK 3 Strategic Thinking or Reasoning	DOK 4 Extended Thinking
Remember Memorize, recognize, recall, locate, identify key terms, concepts, principles	• Recall, recognize, or locate basic facts, terms, details, events, or explicit ideas in texts. • Read words orally in connected text with fluency and accuracy.	Use these Hess CRM curricular examples with most close reading or listening assignments or assessments in any content area.		
Understand Construct a conceptual understanding: clarify, classify, represent, translate, give examples, summarize, infer logical conclusion, predict, explain	• Identify or describe literary elements (e.g., characters, setting). • Select appropriate words when intended meaning or definition is clearly evident. • Describe or explain who, what, where, when, how. • Write simple sentences.	• Specify, explain relationships; explain why (cause and effect). • Give nonexamples or examples. • Summarize results, concepts, ideas. • Make basic inferences or logical predictions from data or texts. • Identify main ideas, accurate generalizations of texts. • Locate information to support central ideas.	• Explain or connect ideas using evidence (e.g., quote, example, text reference). • Make inferences about implicit themes. • Describe how word choice, point of view, or bias may affect the reader's interpretation of a text. • Write a multiparagraph composition for specific purpose, focus, voice, tone, and audience.	• Explain how concepts or ideas specifically relate to other concepts or content domains (e.g., social, political, historical). • Develop generalizations of the results obtained or strategies used and apply them to new problem-based situations.
Apply Carry out or use a procedure in a given situation, carry out (apply to a familiar task) or use a procedure in an unfamiliar or a nonroutine task (transfer)	• Use language structure (prefix-suffix) or word relationships (synonym-antonym) to determine meanings of words. • Apply rules to edit spelling, grammar, punctuation. • Apply format to cite sources.	• Use context to identify intended meaning of words. • Obtain and interpret information using text features. • Apply simple organizational structures to develop paragraphs, sentence types.	• Apply a concept in a new context. • Revise final draft for meaning or progression of ideas. • Apply internal consistency of text organization and structure. • Apply word choice, point of view, style to affect interpretation.	• Illustrate how multiple themes (e.g., historical, geographic, social, artistic, literary) may be interrelated. • Select or devise an approach among many alternatives to research a novel problem.

Analyze Break into constituent parts, determine how parts relate, distinguish, outline, organize, deconstruct (e.g., for bias, point of view, coherence), differentiate between relevant and irrelevant information	• Identify whether specific information is contained in graphic representations (e.g., map, chart, table, diagram) or text features (e.g., caption). • Decide which text structure is appropriate to audience and purpose.	• Categorize or compare literary elements, facts, details, events. • Identify use of literary devices. • Analyze format, organization, or text structures; distinguish between relevant and irrelevant information.	• Analyze information within data sets or within text. • Analyze interrelationships among concepts, issues, problems. • Interpret author's craft (e.g., literary devices, viewpoint) to critique or create a text. • Use reasoning, planning, and evidence to support inferences, theme.	• Analyze multiple sources of evidence from works by the same author or across genres, time periods, or themes. • Analyze complex or abstract themes. • Gather, analyze, and organize multiple information sources. • Analyze multiple discourse styles.
Evaluate Make judgments based on specified criteria, detect inconsistencies or fallacies, judge, critique	**UG:** Unsubstantiated Generalizations = stating an opinion or a claim without providing any support for it!		• Cite evidence and develop a logical argument for conjectures or claims. • Describe, compare, or contrast solution methods. • Verify reasonableness of results.	• Evaluate relevancy, accuracy, and completeness of information drawn from multiple sources. • Apply understanding of interrelated ideas in a novel way, and provide argument or justification for application.
Create Reorganize elements into new patterns or structures, generate, hypothesize, design, plan, produce	• Brainstorm ideas, concepts, problems, or perspectives related to a topic, principle, or concept.	• Generate conjectures or hypotheses based on observations or prior knowledge and experience.	• Synthesize information within one source or text. • Develop a complex model for a given situation. • Develop an alternative solution or ending.	• Synthesize information across multiple sources or texts. • Articulate a new voice, an alternative theme, new knowledge, or a new perspective.

Source: From *Linking Research with Practice: A Local Assessment Toolkit to Guide School Leaders* (p. 6), by K. Hess, 2013, Educational Research in Action. Reprinted with permission.

correct. Unfortunately, a poorly designed classroom assessment will not give you the information you need. The assessment must be actionable.

To paraphrase Frey, Hattie, and Fisher (2018), educators who teach their students how to become assessment-capable learners have students who understand the learning targets, can describe where they are in relation to meeting the success criteria, and can use that information to monitor their progress and select learning strategies to improve the quality of their work (including knowing when and how to seek help). When teachers use daily observable and measurable assessment evidence (what students say, do, and wonder about) and assessment data collected over time (for example, systematic observations, student-led conferences, and interim assessments), they can make meaningful decisions about how best to advance each student's learning.

My Actionable Assessment Cycle (see Figure 1.4) has seven stages.

Stage 1. Clarify learning targets. Start by differentiating between longer-term learning targets (such as unit of study, competency-based goals, and end-of-year expectations) and short-term ones (daily lessons). Consider how a series of learning targets (from least to more complex) fall along a learning continuum to reach the broader learning goal, which you have framed with an essential or a driving question. Use short-cycle assessment activities to address the first learning target of the unit (for example, *I can differentiate between facts and opinions*). More complex learning targets frame activities leading to complex performance tasks (for example, *I can analyze potential bias or credibility of sources in a speech* or *I can compose and support a text-based argument to communicate a message important to me*).

Stage 2. Embed short-cycle formative tasks into instruction. A series of short-cycle actionable assessments—pretests, quick checks for understanding, probing questions, small-group activities, structured discourse, drawing, and graphic organizers—help students build schemas and connect their prior knowledge with new learning. Consider the learning progression as you move from foundational skills (DOK 1) to conceptual understanding (DOK 2) before moving on to strategic or extended thinking, where students will need to integrate multiple skills and concepts in more challenging performance tasks (DOK 3 or 4).

Stage 3. Uncover thinking and document evidence of learning. Document learning evidence fluidly during instruction using everything from class discourse checklists, to conferencing tools, to sketchnotes, to observing dramatic play and all phases of group activities. Metacognition and reflection activities also drive learning forward.

Stage 4. Interpret evidence and frame feedback. With this evidence of learning in hand, analyze the connections students are making when they talk, play, solve problems, draw, write, or use manipulatives. Assessment checkpoints and rubrics designed to describe how learning moves forward are useful tools for students to see where they are now and where they need to go next. Teaching students how to give feedback to their peers and how to self-assess and monitor their own progress increases ownership and the impact of feedback on learning.

FIGURE 1.4
The Actionable Assessment Cycle

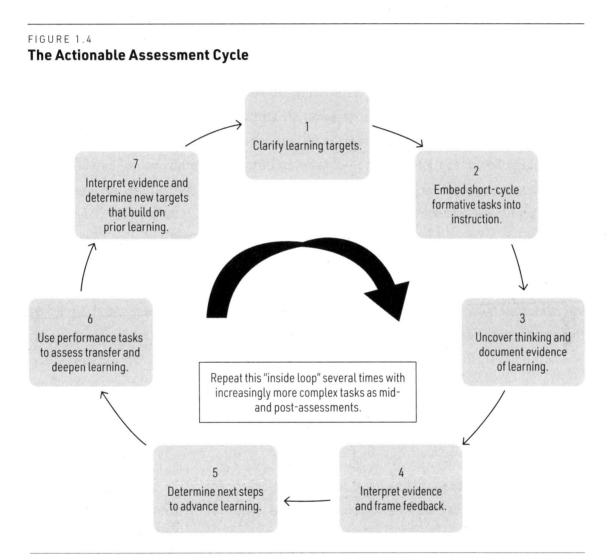

Stage 5. Determine next steps to advance learning. Some students may need additional scaffolding supports—to support language development, executive functioning, or deeper understanding—whereas others might be ready to move on to more complex tasks with minimal modeling or using mentor texts as their guide. Consider which students will

benefit from working one-on-one with the teacher, working with a partner, or working independently. These decisions free up teacher time and focus efforts where they are most needed while giving students more control over their learning. Creating learning menus or station rotations that differentiate tasks provides opportunities for student choice and voice, peer teaching, and short-term goal setting and progress monitoring.

Stage 6. Use performance tasks to assess transfer and deepen learning. Once students have shown progress using short-cycle assessments, it's time to integrate core academic content and personal skills, such as collaboration and self-direction, into assessments that take longer than one or two class periods. These assessments might include performance-based tasks, teacher-guided class projects, student-designed investigations, and peer and self-assessments. Be sure to plan for at least *two rounds of more complex tasks.* This smaller loop within the Actionable Assessment Cycle provides multiple opportunities for students to address the most complex learning targets. Begin with a teacher-guided performance task or self-assessment to model for the class. Next, move to similar small-group tasks with more choice options in the next round. Finally, expand the scope of the assessment tasks to comprise both collaborative and independent components, building in opportunities for peer feedback to improve the quality of student products.

Stage 7. Interpret evidence and determine new targets that build on prior learning. You have now documented student progress along a learning progression with increasing complexity. You will use some of this evidence formatively to document progress and some of it summatively for evidence-based grading and reporting. It's now time to consider how to build on this learning as you move into the next learning and assessment cycle, again applying the five teacher moves (described in Chapters 2–6) to a new unit of study.

To Sum Up

Assessments take many forms, from probing questions, to performance-based tasks, to self-reflections. The primary focus of any assessment is to *advance student learning*. Weaving together the five essential teacher moves creates a coherent Actionable Assessment Cycle that can drive learning forward in any classroom. Let's review those moves now:

1. **A**sk a series of probing questions of increasing complexity.
2. **B**uild schemas in each content area.
3. **C**onsider ways to strategically scaffold learning.
4. **D**esign complex tasks that emphasize transfer and evidence-based solutions.
5. **E**ngage students in metacognition and reflection throughout the learning process.

Now let's look at each of these moves within the Actionable Assessment Cycle. Chapter 2 will focus on the first essential teacher move—asking a series of probing questions.

RELATED RESOURCES

- **Assessment for Learning Project**
  www.assessmentforlearningproject.org

- **Hess Cognitive Rigor Matrices: What Rigor Looks Like in Eight Subject Areas**
  www.karin-hess.com/cognitive-rigor-and-dok

- **Hess Metacognitive Task Cards and Poster: Six Ways to Uncover Thinking and Deepen Understanding**
  www.karin-hess.com/_files/ugd/5e86bd_482328a2c4974063ab79a0b0f09f80ac.pdf

- **Karin Hess's Handy Brain Model (video)**
  www.youtube.com/watch?v=MuHk9GHYnv4

- **Karin Hess on Linking Rigor with Research (video)**
  www.karin-hess.com/free-resources

- **Lucas Foundation Research Briefs on Project-Based Learning and Deeper Learning**
  www.lucasedresearch.org/research/research-briefs

- **"Why Does Memorization Reign Supreme?" by U. J. Hansen (video and article)**
  www.education-reimagined.org/why-memorization-traditional-learning

2

Ask a Series of Probing Questions

Coming up with the right question involves vigorously thinking through the problem, investigating it from various angles, turning closed questions into open-ended ones, and prioritizing which are the most important questions to get at the heart of the matter.

We've been underestimating how well our kids can think.

We see consistently that there are three outcomes [of student-generated questions]. One is that students are more engaged. Second, they take more ownership, which for teachers, this is a huge thing. And the third outcome is they learn more—we see better quality work.

—Dan Rothstein and Luz Santana,
Make Just One Change: Teach Students to Ask Their Own Questions

This chapter focuses on why and how to teach students to use their curiosity to generate questions that will drive and personalize their learning. Why promote a shift from teachers asking all of the questions to teachers encouraging students to ask their own questions? Cognitive science research reminds us that long-term storage of information in the brain depends on the learner making connections and seeing the usefulness of constructing their own meaning (Sousa, 2022). Promoting self-directed learning skills, such as asking questions and using metacognition, empowers learners to transfer learning to new situations.

Why Teach Students the Art of Questioning?

The art of questioning is at the heart of good teaching and deeper learning. More important, if we want students to own their learning, they need to learn how to generate different types of questions for different purposes. When teachers model this approach, students are able to move from less to more complex thinking.

To encourage all students to actively grapple with concepts and freely exchange ideas, teachers must ask a variety of probing questions: *What makes you say that? What evidence can you provide? Would that still be true if…?* Rather than search for that one perfect question to guide your lesson, consider how a series of questions will create a learning pathway to deeper understanding.

Three Ways to Ask a Series of Probing Questions

Asking a variety of questions permeates all stages of the Actionable Assessment Cycle. Teachers can use open-ended essential questions (McTighe & Wiggins, 2013) to frame investigations for a larger unit of study and more focused, but still open-ended, *driving questions* in project-based learning and activities. They can then support these broader questions by asking a series of questions that unpack learning as students delve deeper.

Let's now look at three ways to use a series of *dialogic questions*. Dialogic questions are open-ended, philosophical, and challenging. They promote discussion, critical thinking, and inquiry.

Question Sequencing

This questioning strategy comes from the video titled "The Art of Questioning" from the Teaching Channel (n.d.); the teacher uses it to begin a discussion of a nonfiction text that students have already read independently. In this lesson, a high school English teacher asks a sequence of three types of questions to help students understand informational texts. The teacher first asks the students to personally react to the content (DOK 2); then to interpret the big picture or the underlying meaning or theme (DOK 3); and then to explore how the structure of the text (DOK 2) works to deliver the author's message. Asking students for their personal reaction to content, rather than beginning with a few basic recall questions, engages all students in the discussion right from the start. When students begin to elaborate on their responses using both text-based and personal evidence, they're using deeper thinking. To paraphrase the teacher's comment at the end of the video, "With a sequence of questions, one question leads to the next. So when students are at home by themselves and have to analyze a text, they know the sequence, and they know how to get there on their own by starting small."

Socratic Questioning

Socratic questioning involves teaching students to ask their peers a range of different questions. These include clarification questions (DOK 1) such as, *What do you mean by that?;* assumption-based questions (DOK 2 and 3) such as, *What's the underlying assumption in this message?* or *What does the speaker seem to believe?;* or questions asking for supporting reasoning and evidence, checking credibility of sources, and determining implications and consequences (DOK 3) such as, *What would be the possible effects?* and *What are some of the differing viewpoints?* (DOK 3 and 4).

Student-led Socratic seminars (also called Socratic Circles) put students in greater control of the direction of their own learning, with the teacher acting as a strategic coach. Students split into two groups, with the "outside" group observing the peer-to-peer discussion taking place among the "inside" group. Socratic questioning works in all content areas and grade levels. (See "Related Resources" for a video featuring middle school students engaged in this process.)

Genius Hour

Genius Hour (Spencer, 2020) is a more free-flowing strategy that starts with many student-generated questions that lead to the investigation of a topic of personal or group interest. During 20 percent of instructional time, students work on projects that enable them to pursue their passions, interests, and questions in a creative way. Students then share what they learned with an authentic audience.

A wide range of questions can spark Genius Hour projects. For example, starting with a broad question, such as, *How can I create a video about* _____*?* leads to such questions as these: *What is a storyboard?* (DOK 1); *How can a storyboard help me plan my video?* (DOK 2); *How can I use lighting and camera angles to create a specific mood for my video?* (DOK 3). (For more information on using Genius Hour performance-based assessments, see Chapter 5).

Tips for Effective Questioning

The ultimate goal of modeling how to ask and answer deeper-thinking questions is to teach our students how to formulate their reasoning and become more empowered in the learning process. Students will not become lifelong critical and creative thinkers simply by answering *our* questions.

The following are some tips for engaging learners when posing questions in any setting:

Practice using wait (and think) time. Mary Budd Rowe (1986) authored a literature review on wait time, drawing attention to the amount of time that teachers typically waited for students to respond to their questions. What she found was that teachers typically wait hardly one second between asking a question and calling on a student to answer. This leaves students little time to process the question, draw on prior knowledge, and confidently share a response. For multilingual learners who also need time to translate their response into English (or into another language), responding—and engagement—become almost impossible. Be sure to use wait and think time when posing questions.

Brainstorm without judgment. A second questioning rule of thumb is to generate and record multiple ideas, questions, or responses *before* judging them to be right or wrong. Small groups can use large chart paper with sticky notes (or Jamboard if students are working remotely) to fill the space with ideas. This approach honors everyone's ideas. Often, it's the earlier ideas that lead to more interesting ones later on in the discussion. A good follow-up to brainstorming that deepens understanding is categorizing ideas or identifying the pros and cons of each one.

Ask all students to simultaneously respond, rather than calling on just a few. Teachers can quickly check for understanding in both in-person and virtual classrooms using various hand signals, such as asking students to do thumbs up/thumbs down (I understand/I don't understand) or raise a closed fist (I'm confused) or up to three fingers to show understanding (three fingers = I can explain/teach it to someone else). Response cards can be as simple as displaying A, B, C, or D for four different answer choices or using green light/red light cards for agree/disagree, true/false, and so on.

Model curiosity by making *your* thinking visible. When teachers model thinking aloud to demonstrate their thought processes as they raise novel questions and formulate answers, students see that getting the right answer is less important—and much less interesting—than exploring ideas. Include unique and interesting words in your questions or startling facts and quotations that will automatically pique student interest. For example, *How would a* curmudgeon *respond to this innovation?* or *What about this situation might cause you to* grimace?

Closed and Open-Ended Questions

If you've played the game I Spy or 20 Questions, then you've practiced using closed questions. You can answer closed questions with a "yes" or "no" or by providing memorized definitions, facts, principles, or rules (for example, *Have you ever seen a ghost? Does this model represent a function?*). Closed questions have only one correct answer, even when finding the answer might require multiple steps, as in a math word problem.

Open-ended questions require not only a response, but also an explanation with supporting reasoning and evidence. Open-ended questions can potentially have multiple correct answers (for example, *What lesson can we learn from this story? Is this law fair?*). In a testing situation, we often refer to open-ended questions as *constructed response* because students must construct explanations for their answer using supporting text evidence or explain, say, how a mathematical diagram and calculations support their solution. Open and closed questions serve important but different purposes. (See "Related Resources" for a link to the Right Question Institute, which offers resources for teaching students how to ask and use different types of questions.)

Closed Questions: Surface-Level Understanding

Closed questions are sometimes called *basic* or *surface-level questions*. They have one right answer, which doesn't necessarily mean that they're easy to answer, especially if the student hasn't spent time memorizing the answer. Closed questions tend to be either foundational and procedural recall questions (DOK 1) or conceptual questions (DOK 2). The information needed to answer a closed question is often stated explicitly in the text, or it's derived by applying a routine rule/formula/procedure, recalling a fact or term, or defining a concept (such as *gravity* or *equivalence*).

Basic questions don't take much time to answer because students either know the answer or they don't. Teachers can use fill-in-the-blank or multiple-choice questions or ask students to create a table, label a diagram, or match pairs of items. Because there's only one right answer, basic questions have high test-scoring reliability and are a quick and efficient way to find out if students are acquiring the foundational knowledge they need for learning activities involving near transfer. Dylan Wiliam (2015) suggests that teachers plan their lessons to include "hinge" questions to get on-the-spot evidence about what students do and don't understand to determine who is and isn't ready to move on or who may need additional support and practice.

Although closed questions have an important purpose in lesson planning and assessment, they can only tap into foundational, procedural, and conceptual knowledge (DOK 1 and 2). The greatest limitation of closed questions is that even when students produce the correct answer, it's unclear whether they know more than what we asked for. For example, we may learn that the student can make an accurate observation, but can that same student graph data from observations to see emerging patterns or use observations to generate a new testable question? We shouldn't be satisfied with simply asking different kinds of basic questions. Basic questions are only the first step to deeper explorations of interesting and relevant problems, issues, or themes.

Here's a sampling of basic/closed questions related to recalling terms and concepts. Consider what the student knows if he or she answers these correctly and what deeper understandings about the topic you could ask for next:

- *Can you define _____ or complete the following sentence using one of your vocabulary terms?* (recall a term, fact, or definition [DOK 1])
- *Can you sort these pictures to show examples and nonexamples of _____ ?* (conceptual understanding, compare/contrast [DOK 2])
- *Can you compare and contrast what you know about _____ by completing a Venn diagram?* (conceptual understanding, compare/contrast [DOK 2])
- *Can you demonstrate or explain what happens during _____ (a process or procedure)?* (recall, describe, perform a routine procedure [DOK 1]; explain cause/effect, summarize steps [DOK 2]).

Open-Ended Questions: Toward Deeper Understanding

Open-ended and more rigorous questions uncover important misconceptions and push students to think outside of the box using divergent thinking, building on foundational knowledge. Open-ended questions require responses supported by reasoning:

- *How would you rate these design ideas from the least to most innovative?*
- *What are some of the longest-lasting consequences of this event in history?*

Open-ended questions can also help students fill in gaps in their foundational knowledge. For example, learning the basics of camera shots and video editing will greatly enhance the quality of a student's final video product (for example, *How will changing the lighting or camera angle create different moods for this scene? What shots will achieve your intended mood?*). Rigorous questions not only spark deeper understanding, but also can lead to both metacognitive and reflective thinking.

Planning Your Questions at Different DOK Levels

Most educators have not had as many strong models for asking open-ended questions as we have had for asking closed questions. Deeper questions take more time to develop, more time for students to answer, and certainly more time to correct. Responding to deeper questions requires students to provide evidence to support their analyses, inferences, conclusions, or perspectives.

To develop deeper questions and tasks that will uncover *how* students figured out an answer, we need to consider what prior knowledge or experience they can bring to the question at hand—that is, what learning might transfer from earlier lessons and what learning might transfer from this lesson to future lessons. In other words, these questions are part of a learning trajectory intended to deepen understanding over time.

One strategy for generating a range of questions at different complexity levels is to begin with a blank cognitive rigor matrix template, filling in questions at different DOK levels that might logically connect foundational understanding with deeper thinking during learning. (You can use the format shown in Figure 2.1.) Some questions will be more like snorkeling (on the surface) and others more like scuba diving (in deeper waters).

Figure 2.1 frames a hypothetical unit of study with a broad statement of enduring understanding: *The traditions of a group of people are influenced by their history, place of origin, and culture.* This understanding generates a variety of questions for exploration and learning, from DOK 1 (*What are some of your family's traditions?*) to DOK 4 (*Can culture or traditions create conflicts among groups of people?*).

Wiggins and McTighe (2005) describe *enduring understandings* as the insights a learner gains by making connections and integrating new knowledge into existing understandings. Enduring understandings summarize important concepts and core processes that have lasting value beyond the classroom. Teachers should use these to develop one or more essential questions to guide student inquiry. Essential questions will typically be at the DOK 4 level—extended thinking.

Note that all cells of the matrix shown in Figure 2.1 are, by design, *not* filled in. The purpose of this planning is simply to generate a few possible ways to help students begin to make connections at different DOK levels and to maximize their engagement. Class discourse will surely generate more questions that are relevant to students.

When teachers plan their questions, learning deepens. Questions spark the brain to make connections and solidify learning. They help learners probe for deeper understanding and create interpersonal and intrapersonal feedback loops that drive not only learning, but also the motivation to learn. Hattie (2012) found that in classrooms where dialogue is routine, student achievement gains are more than twice as great as we might expect for one year of schooling (0.40), with an effect size of 0.82.

FIGURE 2.1
Generating Questions at Differing Complexity/DOK Levels

Sample enduring understanding for the unit: The traditions of a group of people are influenced by their history, place of origin, and culture.				
Depth of Knowledge and Types of Thinking	**DOK 1**	**DOK 2**	**DOK 3**	**DOK 4**
Remember	What is a tradition? What is culture?			
Understand	What are some of your family's traditions?	How are culture, history, and traditions related?		
Apply			How does your family's history and culture influence your traditions?	
Analyze		What are the pros and cons of adopting new traditions?		**Essential question:** Can culture or traditions create conflicts among groups of people?
Evaluate			Do you have a family tradition that does *not* reflect your history or culture?	**Essential question:** Does mass immigration to a new country affect the culture and traditions of those groups of people?
Create	What questions do you have about your traditions?		How could you merge two traditions into something new and meaningful?	

Applying Questioning Strategies in the Actionable Assessment Cycle

With the stages of the Actionable Assessment Cycle in mind, let's look at how teachers can use a variety of questioning techniques to clarify learning targets, embed short-cycle formative tasks into instruction, uncover thinking and document evidence of learning, interpret evidence and frame feedback, determine next steps to advance learning, and use performance tasks to assess transfer and deepen learning.

Stage 1. Clarify learning targets.

Teachers can clarify learning targets by using essential and driving questions.

Essential Questions

Wiggins and McTighe (2005) operationalized the use of enduring understandings and essential questions in what they called *backward design*. Teachers ask a broad, open-ended essential question to frame learning activities and spark more questions for study during a unit or even across grade levels. For example, the essential question, *How does* where *you live influence* how *you live?* could work in social studies and science classes at many grade levels. Essential questions arise from related statements of enduring understanding, such as, "The geography, climate, and natural resources of a region influence the economy and lifestyle of the people living there" (McTighe & Wiggins, 2013, p. 5), and they have many different possible answers.

Essential questions do the following:

- Stimulate ongoing thinking and inquiry.
- Raise more questions.
- Spark discussion and debate.
- Are asked and re-asked throughout the unit (and maybe the year).
- Demand justification and support.
- Generate answers that change as understanding deepens. (Based on McTighe & Wiggins, 2013)

Driving Questions

Driving questions are open-ended, designed specifically to guide project-based learning (PBL) investigations. PBLs have several of the following common characteristics:

- A driving question that hooks student interest
- An entry event that provides real-world context and background
- Learning that involves application of core academic and personal skills
- Learning that requires collaboration with peers
- Multifaceted forms of assessment (processes, products, and self-reflection)
- Learning that involves public sharing

In her video titled "Writing Driving Questions," author and educator April Smith (2017) defines a driving question as the overall question a teacher poses to students to guide them through a problem or process. Although the skills needed to complete the project are driven by academic standards, the standards are not explicitly stated in the driving question. Smith presents a simple three-part model as the starting point for developing action-oriented driving questions:

Who is responsible? + Who is the authentic audience? + What is the problem or challenge?

Example: How can (I/we) + help the people in my school or community + stay safe during a natural disaster?

Here are some examples of driving questions with connections to real-world problems or issues:

- *Why do we need (bees, water, human rights, technology)? How can we teach others about its importance?*
- *What can we do to save an endangered species? How can we involve others to take action with us?*
- *How can we predict the size of a population in 50 years, and what are some implications for the planet?*
- *Can fake news cause harm? How can we help others detect and do something about the spread of fake news?*

Stage 2. Embed short-cycle formative tasks into instruction.

Teachers frequently use short-cycle formative questions and tasks to pre-assess background knowledge and reinforce discourse skills. Many of these naturally build in wait and think time. They can tap emotional engagement: *What's one word or picture to describe how you're feeling today? How would you like to work on this task, alone or in a group?* They can also tap cognitive engagement: *How would you describe the mood of the poem? What process or operation could you use to solve this?*

Let's look at a variety of questioning tools at this stage of the Actionable Assessment Cycle.

Think-Pair-Share and Think-Pair-Square

These Spencer Kagan (1992) strategies are familiar to many educators. When I first learned the strategies in a workshop with Kagan, he identified three key purposes: allow for wait time, encourage simultaneous engagement, and hold each student accountable by making their thinking visible.

The teacher begins by posing an inferential or a decision-making question, such as, *What does this statement or symbol imply? Which solution is correct and why?* Individual students *think* and respond by writing, drawing, or manipulating materials. Next, students *pair* up and *share* ideas. At this point, the teacher encourages students to refine, merge, change, or add to their ideas. In the final step, each pair joins another pair to make a *square*, where students once again compare and finalize their collaborative response. To add movement to the pairing before sharing, Love and Strobaugh (2018) offer a variation of this strategy called Mingle-Pair-Share. Students move about the room while music plays; when the music stops, they partner with a student nearby to share ideas.

Starting with think time for retrieval practice requires students to recall information *on their own*. If teachers ask students to recall information in pairs or groups, some students will miss the chance to strengthen their memory of the material. The small-group discussions that follow are excellent preparation for whole-class dialogue or for one group to summarize for or "teach" the rest of the class. Using breakout rooms during remote learning is an effective way to enable pairs and squares to work together.

Camera Off/Camera On

When working in virtual environments, students turn off their laptop or cell phone cameras while the teacher poses a question. After about 5–10 seconds, students who are ready to respond turn their cameras back on. Each student who still has their camera off poses a follow-up question to someone who has shared a response. Teachers sometimes like to provide a few question stems to help the "prober" group with their follow-up questions (for example, *Can you add a little more about…? Why do you think…? Is this a problem for everyone?*).

Wait and Waterfall

The teacher poses a question and students either select a provided answer card (for example, true/false) or write their responses on a whiteboard or, in a virtual environment, in the chat box. Students hold up their answers or push "send" only when the questioner says, "Waterfall"! Then everyone responds at the same time, holding up their responses for about 30 seconds. Students take time to skim and discuss responses, looking to see who agrees with them or whether there are patterns in the responses (for example, *Most of the class thought this was true because…*). As with Think-Pair-Share, each individual student gets retrieval practice time at the start of this activity and can later integrate ideas after hearing the ideas of their peers.

Word Clouds

Word clouds visually represent information or survey data, using the size of the text font to show the frequency—or the popularity—of an idea. Word clouds quickly show differing perspectives, trends, or ideas related to a topic or question without requiring a lot of background reading. Drawing inferences from word clouds can lead to new questions and deeper discussions. Word cloud generating tools—such as Mentimeter (www .mentimeter.com), WordItOut (www.worditout.com), and Word Clouds (www.wordclouds. com)—can easily create word clouds for both emotional and cognitive engagement purposes (for example, to respond to such questions as, *Which is your favorite season? What's your best strategy when figuring out word meaning? What is liberty?*). (For more ways to use the Word Clouds strategy, check out the article by Monica Burns in "Related Resources.")

See-Think-Wonder

Teachers often use this quick question-generating strategy after students observe a demonstration, examine a picture, or view a video clip. Students fill in three sections of a graphic organizer: They describe what they see (a visual of an eye or a magnifying glass identifies this section); they interpret what they think it means (a thinking cloud visual identifies this section); and they generate questions they now wonder about (a question mark identifies this section). Large- and small-group discussions follow the See-Think-Wonder activity.

"Funnel" Your Questions

Teachers can implement this gamelike strategy using a sequence of broader to narrower questions, like a funnel with a wide end and a narrow end. The purpose of funneling is to uncover information, such as to solve a mystery event or figure out how someone corrected the solution to a math challenge; each subsequent question asks for greater detail. The first group poses a broad general question to the second group (for example, *Was this a real or a fictional event? Did you find an error in the graphing?*). After someone on the team responds, the first team follows up with another question to narrow the focus (for example, *What was the time period or setting? Was it a calculation error or an error in the intervals used?*). Questions keep narrowing until they uncover enough information and details for a team to solve the mystery.

Turn-and-Talk Frames

Instead of using exit cards at the end of a lesson, stop every 12–15 minutes during a lesson to enable students to make a personal connection and consolidate their learning before going on with turn-and-talk frames. Turn-and-talk frames refer to questions or comments on cards that ask students for a response (like the six examples in Figure 2.2). Only a short amount of time is needed (30 seconds to 2 minutes) to engage every student and multiple brain lobes by asking students to respond using a combination of drawing, writing, or talking. The questions that appear on the cards range from DOK 1 (quick recall), to DOK 2 (conceptual, observational), to DOK 3 (requiring reasoning and support). Students can also write their names on the cards for you to collect at the end of the lesson. Some teachers suggest having students add their responses in their personal learning journals. Turn-and-talk frames work well as quick pre-post assessments, individual reflections, checks for understanding, and preparation for small-group and class discussions. For remote learning, you can use tools such as Padlet and Jamboard to collect individual or small-group responses electronically.

Wonder Walls

To generate interest in starting a new unit of study or launching a PBL project, teachers can ask students to create a wonder wall bulletin board using student-generated questions. These questions can become the first step to a deeper-level project and could be at any DOK level. (See "Related Resources" for a link to the Doing Good Together website, which features ideas for helping students generate questions for Wonder Walls.)

KWHL Charts

A well-planned lesson or unit of study should begin with a pre-assessment aligned with some—but not necessarily all—aspects of the unit's learning targets. Pre-assessments can be informal, such as asking small groups to brainstorm how they might find information on a topic using a key word search on the internet. Or students might use a KWHL chart to explore a topic. Although many educators are already familiar with "KWL" (what I **K**now, **W**onder, **L**earned), I always add the "H" question (**H**ow?) to spark thinking about the ways students could investigate their questions, such as by asking an expert, building and testing a prototype, or going on a field trip. KWHL charts can provide useful information to the teacher about what students already know and what topics might need direct instruction or strategic coaching. Here's what it looks like in terms of DOK levels:

K: *What do you know about this topic or issue?* (DOK 1)

W: *What do you wonder about, what would you like to learn, or what questions will your report answer?* (DOK 1 or 2)

H: *How can you find the answers to these questions?* (DOK 1, 2, or 3)

L: *How can you reflect on, summarize, or share what you have learned?* (DOK 1, 2, or 3)

FIGURE 2.2
Sample Turn-and-Talk Frames

Note: These samples can be cut apart and used for quick responses

Two-Minute Interview	Define and Draw It	Three Things I Know About _____
My name:	List a key word or idea:	1. (before the lesson)
My partner's name:		
My question:		
My partner's responses:	What does it mean?	2. (by the middle of the lesson)
What was the most important idea you heard so far?		
	Draw something to help you remember it.	3. (by the end of the lesson)
What's a supporting detail for that idea?		

Check Your Prediction	Observe-Think-Wonder	Question of the Day
What will you read, try, listen to, or watch?	I saw/heard _____.	My name:
		Question for today's lesson:
My prediction:		
	That made me think _____.	Stop three times to add to or revise your response and use supporting details.
Why do I think so?		
		1.
	Now I wonder _____.	
On the other side of this card, describe or draw and label what really happened.		2.
		3.

Media/Artifact Search

This is an extension of a strategy I used when teaching middle school. With "photo search," I showed students a famous historical photograph—Orville and Wilbur Wright at Kitty Hawk—and asked, "Who are these brothers and why do we remember them?" The initial questions get the students started asking more questions and researching the answer (for example, *Who is in the photo, and what are they doing? Where/when was this photo taken?*). The answers should not be obvious and require citing a source with supporting evidence. You can use Media/Artifact Search with visuals (a video, a photo, paintings), historical artifacts, or objects. Students draw on their combined prior knowledge and then decide which clues will help them investigate further. Students generate a number of new and interesting questions to get to the answer, and they're excited when they finally solve the mystery and actually find the photo during their search. This is an excellent strategy to promote ownership when introducing such research skills as triangulating information from multiple sources. You can also use Jamboards to capture and categorize initial class or group knowledge and ideas before conducting the research. (See "Related Resources" for links to the Smithsonian and PBS Learning Media websites.)

Stage 3. Uncover thinking and document evidence of learning.

Uncovering thinking with peer-to-peer discourse helps establish a community of inquiry and problem solving where students learn to share their thoughts freely and respect the ideas of others. Collaboration and teamwork activities are threads that support all of the five essential teacher moves.

Teachers can use several questioning strategies, such as teacher-designed hinge questions and student-led Socratic Circles, to uncover thinking and document evidence of learning. Here are a few additional strategies that you might find useful.

Send a Question or (Incorrect) Solution

I adapted this strategy from Spencer Kagan's "Send a Problem" structure (1992). It promotes team building, and you can use it to review what students have already learned (DOK 1 or 2) or to teach them to ask more open-ended questions (DOK 3). Each team starts by putting their heads together for a few minutes to develop a question or problem for another team to answer or solve, or a solution to a problem that includes an error. Before sharing with the next team, the first team must draft an acceptable response to their question. Then they send the question or solution to the next team to answer. When time is called, the second team sends their response back for correction and feedback. Teams must not only answer the questions they've generated, but also teach the other team how to find the answer if those students get stuck or solve the problem incorrectly. I've also used this approach for sending "sample evidence" to a group. The receiving group must judge the quality of the suggested evidence in supporting a stated claim. In remote classrooms, teachers can use a Google slide deck, with a slide for each team's question and breakout rooms for team discussions.

Would You Rather?

The purpose of this open-ended questioning strategy is to offer choices with no intended correct answer. After making their choice, students share and support it with reasoning. For example, in grades 6–8, students see a picture of paper money along with the question, *Would you rather make $50,000 a year when everyone around you makes $25,000 a year or make $100,000 a year when everyone around you makes $200,000 a year?* Whichever option the students choose, they must justify their reasoning using mathematics. Would You Rather Math provides some great examples of teacher-developed math questions for students in grades K–12 (see "Related Resources").

This or That?

This-or-that questions also offer choices in a variety of subject areas, such as events in history, literature, and science. You can use them to describe personal choices, such as, *Would you prefer to read this—a graphic novel—or that—a chapter book? Are you more like this—a graphic artist—or that—a sculptor?*

Picture Talks and Math Talks

Many elementary teachers already use visuals of real-world objects, such as eggs in a carton or coins in groups, to spark math talks that draw out students' prior knowledge and build background knowledge for an upcoming lesson. Students then apply these concepts to solve new problems or tasks. Picture talk questions run the gamut from simple to more complex open-ended questions. You might show two pictures to students—of vehicles, animals, plants, and so on—and ask them whether the main character is more like this one or more like that one. Matching unlike ideas promotes metaphoric thinking and abstract reasoning.

Formative Assessment Probes

Keeley and colleagues (2008) have mastered the art of asking questions that probe conceptual understanding and uncover common misconceptions in science. Each probe begins with a short scenario or visual (for example, a graph, an unlabeled diagram) followed by a question, such as, *What happened to this fruit to make it rot?* Some probes ask students to choose from the options or explanations given, whereas others ask for explanations with supporting evidence. Because these probes have been field-tested with students at different grade levels, each probe provides insights into how to interpret typical responses from elementary, middle, or high school students and suggests next steps for instruction.

Four Corners

You can use this strategy with open-ended questions that have multiple possible responses. The purpose is to uncover differing perspectives on a problem or issue. Divide your classroom into four areas (or, online, into four virtual breakout rooms) where students gather to discuss the ideas they have in common in response to a question (for example, *Which of these foods is the healthiest and why?*). You can pre-assign students to different perspectives, have students choose a statement they most strongly agree with, or allow students to mingle and form their own discussion groups.

Inside-Outside Circles

This strategy also begins with an open-ended question such as, *How does this writer engage the audience?* Half of the students form an outside circle facing a partner who is part of an inside circle. Students share ideas with the partner for two to three minutes. When time is called, everyone moves to the next partner, where they paraphrase what they've already heard and add their thoughts. This activity (run like speed dating) only takes as much time as you want it to take. In other words, students don't need to pair up with every student in the class. A few rounds of pairing will be adequate to uncover differing ideas.

Value Lines (Taking a Stand)

This is another strategy that begins with an open-ended statement having multiple possible interpretations. The teacher poses a broad claim or statement (similar to an enduring understanding) to the class (for example, *There are many benefits to having open borders* or *Confederate monuments should be removed*). Individuals decide to what degree they agree with this statement, and they write a percentage representing their agreement (100 percent = strongly agree, 75 percent = agree). The class then forms a value line that stretches from 100 percent agreement to 0 percent agreement. Each student discusses with those on either side of them why they landed in that place on the line. After everyone has shared their similar perspectives, representatives from sections of the line summarize everyone's reasoning for agreeing or disagreeing. This interactive activity can set the stage for building arguments and counterarguments on a topic. For younger classes, or during remote learning, students can hold up one of three cards with a happy face, neutral face, or disagree face.

Barometer (Taking a Stand)

This strategy is similar to the value line in that it begins with an open-ended statement and asks students to take a stand, creating a range—or barometer—for their responses. Individual students respond to a broad statement from the teacher, choosing strongly agree, agree, disagree, or strongly disagree. Or students can write a short response in their learning journals and then determine where their opinions fall along the barometer. The organization Facing History and Ourselves suggests making a contract with students beforehand that reiterates class rules about respecting the opinions of others and calls for students to be honest but polite when responding.

Stages 4 and 5. Interpret evidence and frame feedback; determine next steps to advance learning.

The seminal work of Black and Wiliam (1998) pushed educators to rethink how to structure giving feedback, including actively engaging students in the learning process when they self-assess, reflect, and set personal goals for learning. Let's now look at some questioning strategies that are useful for conferencing and student self-reflection. Two are teacher directed and the other is teacher facilitated, with students taking the lead. (Chapter 6 offers more ways to engage students in metacognition and reflection activities.)

5-Minute Teacher–Student Writing Conferences

High school English teacher Jori Krulder (2018) devised this efficient way to manage time to meet with all of her students during class. Before the one-on-one conferences, she skims student essays and makes notes. She then hands back the unmarked papers for students to reflect on using a few targeted questions such as, *What score would you give your essay, and why? How would you like to improve your essay?* In addition to scoring their own papers, students choose a growth area they want to discuss and work on. After the conference, students explain their plans for revision. This strategy accomplishes several purposes: student self-assessment, self-reflection, and goal setting.

Online Teacher–Student Conferencing

Krulder (2020) also discusses how she made the transition from in-person to remote conferencing with her students about books they were reading independently. She placed students in individual breakout rooms during their daily 15-minute reading time. Each day, she joined a few different rooms to have a one-on-one discussion with students, using the same questions she normally used for in-class conferencing. This systematic online conferencing strategy could work for any content area and doesn't disrupt the rest of the class.

20-Minute Peer Feedback System

Author and PBL expert John Spencer (2015) suggests using a five-step process for peers to give and get feedback on products or processes they're working on. In the following list, sample questions like those in 1, 2, and 5 reflect what a peer might ask to better understand another student's project. Sample questions like those in 3 and 4 can help the receiver of feedback to better understand the suggestions from peers.

1. Pitching (*Can you explain your idea? What are you working on?*)
2. Clarifying (*Is this what you mean? Are we correct in thinking you are trying to ___?*)
3. Offering feedback (*Do you have any suggestions for me?*)
4. Paraphrasing (*Is this what you're suggesting? Do you think I/we should ___?*)
5. Coming up with next steps (*What do you plan to do next?*)

Each step takes only two minutes. This strategy turns more control over to the students to guide their conferencing time, freeing up the teacher to provide support as needed. (See "Related Resources" for a link to Spencer's directions for the 20-minute peer feedback system.)

Stage 6. Use performance tasks to assess transfer and deepen learning.

Performance-based assessments include a range of ways that students can demonstrate their learning by actually *doing*—by building, creating, writing, and performing using authentic (real-world) skills. This continuum begins with smaller performance-based assessments—such as short-cycle diagnostic tasks and course-embedded guided performance tasks—that gradually lead to more complex project-based learning units and extended tasks, like capstones. Figure 2.3 shows this continuum.

To Sum Up

You can use many of the questioning strategies discussed here, such as Wonder Walls, Socratic Circles, and conferencing, to build deeper content knowledge *before* launching performance-based inquiry, project-based learning, or Genius Hours. Figure 2.4 summarizes some of the ways you can apply the strategies described in this chapter throughout the learning process to deepen understanding and uncover thinking.

In the next chapter, we will consider the second essential teacher move: building schemas in each content area.

FIGURE 2.3
Performance Assessment Continuum

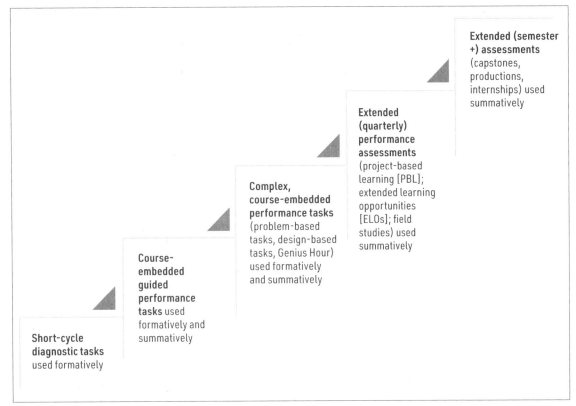

Extended (semester
+) assessments
(capstones,
productions,
internships) used
summatively

Extended
(quarterly)
performance
assessments
(project-based
learning [PBL];
extended learning
opportunities
[ELOs]; field
studies) used
summatively

Complex,
course-embedded
performance tasks
(problem-based
tasks, design-based
tasks, Genius Hour)
used formatively
and summatively

Course-
embedded
guided
performance
tasks used
formatively and
summatively

Short-cycle
diagnostic tasks
used formatively

Source: From *A Local Assessment Toolkit to Promote Deeper Learning* (p. 133), by K. Hess, 2018, Corwin. Adapted with permission.

RELATED RESOURCES

- **"The 20-Minute Peer Feedback System"**
  www.spencerauthor.com/the-20-minute-peer-feedback-system

- **"Better Questions in the Classroom Lead Students to Think Harder—And Learn Deeper" by S. Bradbury and R. Berlin**
  www.edsurge.com/news/2021-06-28-better-questions-in-the-classroom-lead-students-to-think-harder
  -and-learn-deeper

- **Facing History and Ourselves Teaching (strategies, resources, and videos)**
  www.facinghistory.org
  - **Barometer (A Teaching Strategy): Taking a Stand on Controversial Issues**
    www.facinghistory.org/resource-library/teaching-strategies/
    barometer-taking-stand-controversial-issues
  - **Taking Barometer Online**
    www.facinghistory.org/resource-library/video/taking-barometer-online

- **"Five Ways to Use Word Clouds in the Classroom" by Monica Burns**
  www.edutopia.org/article/5-ways-use-word-clouds-classroom

- **"How to Write Driving Questions for Project-Based Learning" by April Smith (video)**
  www.youtube.com/watch?v=u0Eojnkb3Gs

- **Media Images Library compiled by media literacy consultant Frank Baker**
  www.middleweb.com/author/frankwbaker

- **PBS Learning Media**
  www.vermont.pbslearningmedia.org

- **Right Question Institute**
  www.rightquestion.org

- **"Scaffolding Discussion Skills with a Socratic Circle" (video)**
  www.edutopia.org/video/scaffolding-discussion-skills-socratic-circle

- **Smithsonian Institute Archives**
  https://siarchives.si.edu/what-we-do/photograph-and-image-collections

- **Wonder Walls**
  www.doinggoodtogether.org/bhf/create-a-wonder-wall

- **Would You Rather Math**
  www.wouldyourathermath.com

FIGURE 2.4
Actionable Strategies for Asking Probing Questions

Actionable Assessment Cycle Stages	Questioning Strategies	Primary Purpose	Look Fors: Students answer, investigate, and generate questions
1. Clarify learning targets.	Essential Questions and Enduring Understandings	Frame a unit of study or plan a lesson focus.	• What makes an artist, a musician, or a dancer great? • What makes a message or argument compelling? • Why should governments have a balance of power?
	Driving Questions	Launch project-based learning (PBL).	• How can we take action about _____ and share what we've learned?
2. Embed short-cycle formative tasks.	Think-Pair-Share and Think-Pair-Square	Reinforce and solidify learning; prepare for discussion.	• Do you agree? • Can you find an error or design flaw?

Actionable Assessment Cycle Stages	Questioning Strategies	Primary Purpose	Look Fors: Students answer, investigate, and generate questions
2. Embed short-cycle formative tasks. (*continued*)	Turn-and-Talk Frames	Reinforce and solidify learning (vocabulary, language, math skills).	• What are three examples of _____? • What was most difficult and why? • Can you draw it?
	Wonder Walls	Respond to topics, interests, data, artifacts, photos, current events, and so on.	• What would you like to know? • What are you curious about?
	Know, Wonder, How, Learn (KWHL)	Generate background knowledge and interest related to a topic.	• What do I already *know*? • What do I *wonder*? • *How* can I find out more? • What did I *learn*?
	Word Clouds	Identify differing perspectives; explore and interpret related ideas.	• How do you feel about this? • What is the main reason why? • What phrase sums up the theme?
	Funnel Questions	Ask related questions that drill down to build a knowledge base, with each question building on the previous response.	• Did this event take place before _____? • Did it take place in our country? • What event led up to or caused this to happen?
	Media/Artifact Search	Practice research skills; locate sources and document supporting evidence.	• What event (or who) is depicted? • What year do you think this occurred? • Can you find at least three supporting sources for your ideas?
3. Uncover thinking and document evidence of learning.	Hinge Questions	Build questions (procedural, factual, conceptual) into lesson plans to determine whether students are ready to move forward.	• Which is a true statement about photosynthesis? • Why do you need to combine like terms before _____?
	Send a Question or (Incorrect) Solution	Review learning with student-generated questions (or answers); peer teaching.	• Which solution is correct? Can you prove it? • Is the claim supported by _____?
	Would You Rather? This or That?	Develop concepts, apply background knowledge and supporting reasoning or evidence.	• Which do you choose? Explain your reasoning.
	Picture Talks and Math Talks	Practice explaining reasoning, making connections to concepts.	• Does this scene depict one-point perspective? Why or why not? • Can you write an equation for this relationship?
	Formative Assessment Probes	Develop concepts and identify misconceptions; apply reasoning using supporting evidence.	• Which interpretation of the graph is accurate and why? • Which examples describe chemical changes? How do you know?

(*continued*)

FIGURE 2.4
Actionable Strategies for Asking Probing Questions (*continued*)

Actionable Assessment Cycle Stages	Questioning Strategies	Primary Purpose	Look Fors: Students answer, investigate, and generate questions
3. Uncover thinking and document evidence of learning. (*continued*)	Four Corners Inside-Outside circles Value Lines Barometer	Practice collaborative discourse when confronting controversial topics or issues; building arguments and counterarguments.	• How strongly do you agree with this statement? • With whose opinion in this article do you most agree?
	Question Sequencing	Initially respond to and interpret texts.	• Can you react to the text on a personal level? • What is the author's message or theme? • How is the text structured?
	Socratic Circles	Practice collaborative discourse, identifying multiple perspectives; supporting reasoning with evidence; providing peer feedback.	• How can you verify or disprove that assumption? • What are you implying? • What would be an alternative?
4. Interpret evidence and frame feedback. *and* **5. Determine next steps to advance learning.**	Metacognitive Task Cards	Provide self- or peer metacognitive prompts.	• What connections are you making? • What is your group's plan and roles? • What new ideas or questions has this raised for you?
	5-Minute Teacher–Student Writing Conferences Online Teacher–Student Conferencing	Practice self-reflection, self-assessment, goal setting.	• What score would you give ____ and why? • How would you like to improve?
	20-Minute Peer Feedback System	Have peers give and receive feedback while working on projects.	• Can you clarify that? • Is this what you mean? • Can you provide an example?
6. Use performance tasks to assess transfer and deepen learning.	Problem-Based Performance Tasks	Create a scenario or challenge with options for student choice and voice.	• What resources are available for working on this challenge? • What final product or performance will demonstrate what we've learned?
	Inquiry-Based Learning	Ask teams to use driving questions to initiate investigations.	• How can we share what we've learned about ____ with an authentic audience?
	Genius Hour	Ask students to generate questions to guide investigations.	• What am I curious about? • What do I want to learn? • How can I ____?

3

Build Schemas

You can think of a schema as a sort of uber neural pattern—a set of neural shelves that students can easily set new ideas on. Why so easily? Because students have practiced enough with the material that their minds have begun to integrate common patterns. Schemas tie together the different concepts that a student is studying, including both procedural and declarative components. Schemas are the quintessential form of prior knowledge…. Schemas shape our thoughts about what we are learning… and allow new learning to be more easily placed in with other, previously learned material.

—Barbara Oakley, Beth Rogowsky, and Terrance Sejnowski,
Uncommon Sense Teaching: Practical Insights in Brain Science to Help Students Learn

Several years ago, I was working with educators in Santa Clara, California. After three full days of workshops, they jokingly told me that if they wanted to email me in the future, they would put the word *schema* in the subject line because they knew it was so important to me that I'd have to read their message. Building schemas *is* really important, yet in my experience, many teachers do not address it with intent when planning instruction. Schemas allow chess experts to quickly master new chess patterns or high-level athletes to effectively integrate more complex skills to up the quality of their game. Schemas become frameworks for learning new content and dramatically expanding a learner's knowledge base.

Why Build Schemas?

Seminal work on schemas and problem solving (Newell & Simon, 1972) identifies what expert learners possess that novice learners lack—schemas that enable them to categorize a problem, construct mental representations, search for appropriate problem-solving strategies, evaluate the strategies, and store information for later use.

Performing a new procedure or making sense of new content uses a lot of working memory space when there's no schema to connect with. The new information often doesn't "stick"—that is, it doesn't get into the neocortex for you to apply in different ways—because of the hippocampus. The latter organ blocks learning when negative associations interfere and has no way to organize information, discern relevant from irrelevant information, or connect and consolidate new ideas. "In fact, the stronger the schema, the less likely the hippocampus is involved" (Oakley et al., 2021, p. 147). As in a Monopoly game, when you have built strong schemas, you can "pass Go" (the hippocampus) and "collect $200" (process and store the new learning).

Learning activities that build schemas (mental models) in each content domain is crucial to students' long-term memory retrieval and their ability to transfer learning to novel situations (far transfer). To build schemas, teachers can use a variety of strategies that focus on conceptual understanding (DOK 2): differentiating examples from nonexamples, using visual displays and models that show how parts relate to the whole, and asking questions that reflect substantive understanding of concepts or challenge misconceptions.

Building a schema involves integrating declarative knowledge (content) and procedural knowledge (skills and strategies) (Goodwin, 2017). To guide students in building content-specific schemas, a teacher must consider four questions:

- What are the unifying concepts (declarative knowledge) and essential skills (procedural knowledge) of this discipline? Enduring understandings for units of study include broadly stated unifying concepts and essential skills. So begin with those understandings or your essential questions.

- How do the parts (concepts, skills, and structures) relate to the whole (for example, math problem solving, graphic design processes, writing and text genres, body systems)?

- What prior knowledge—that is, earlier schemas and patterns—do students already have that they can build on or that might actually confuse them when new information is introduced?

- What common misconceptions might students have that you may need to address? (Chapter 2 describes formative assessment probes designed to uncover misconceptions.)

Sometimes, in our effort to create clear and simplistic examples during instruction, we inadvertently make later learning more confusing, resulting in misconceptions. Take the example of how we have taught fractions in the past; we say there's a number on the top and a number on the bottom, when actually a fraction isn't two numbers, but one number that is smaller than (or part of) the number one. Or consider what we say when we teach students to subtract—that you can't take a larger number from a smaller number, only to find out that you actually can. The result is a negative number (as when the temperature drops below zero).

Building on an Existing Schema

Whether you're introducing a completely new mental model or building on an existing one, being clear and unambiguous is a good rule of thumb. Two of the most common ways we build a schema are to have some mental models that help us understand how to *organize and structure* information and others that help us use procedures to *process* information. Mental models draw on prior stored knowledge, such as knowing the structure of narrative writing or the process of tackling a math word problem.

Let's look at how we can use an existing schema to build a more sophisticated one. The two examples that follow show a structural schema for teaching text genres and a procedural schema for mathematics problem solving.

Building a Structural Schema

Reading and writing in the primary grades emphasize building schemas for narratives and stories. A simple schema that many K–1 teachers use when they discuss stories is the SWBS Chart (see Figure 3.1): **S**omebody (a character) + **W**anted (to have or do something) + **B**ut (that caused a problem) + **S**o this is how the problem was resolved. SWBS helps to not only introduce new vocabulary but also connect the vocabulary familiar to students with genre-specific terms (for example, somebody = character; wanted = motivation). As you can see in Figure 3.1, filling in the different categories on the SWBS chart when discussing stories builds mental patterns about the parts of *all* stories and narrative poems. Before students can fluently write words, a teacher might ask them to draw (to sketchnote) key information in each cell of the chart; this will also help them practice a similar schema for oral retelling and summarizing later on. Eventually, the class reads stories together and discusses what to write in each cell. When students begin to write their own stories, they now have a simple schema, or framework, to guide them in knowing what to include. The SWBS chart can also serve as a prewriting planning tool or a peer conferencing feedback tool.

FIGURE 3.1

Using an SWBS Chart to Build Schemas: Story Structure Patterns

Title of Story and Author	Somebody Who?	Wanted Something?	But There was a problem.	So What happened?
The Mitten by Jan Brett	A boy named Nick asked his grandma	for mittens as white as snow.	He dropped one mitten in the snow and couldn't find it because it was white.	Lots of animals crawled into the mitten, stretching it until a bear sneezed and sent it flying into the air. Then Nick found it.
Journey by Aaron Becker	A girl is very bored.	She wants someone to play with her.	Everyone is too busy to play.	She finds a magic crayon and draws places she wants to go and then travels there. At the end of her journey, she returns home.
Your story title:				

As students fill in the chart each day, general patterns for all narratives emerge. The SWBS chart is clear and simple and can be expanded upon over time as the narratives that students read and write become more complex. Teachers can integrate more genre-specific vocabulary (part of a schema) as the visual chart evolves to include more sophisticated information, such as setting, dialogue, protagonist, conflict, theme, and so on.

The SWBS schema is helpful only when reading or writing *narratives*. We know from research (Hess, 2018a) that the readers who struggle the most tend to internalize a narrative schema and then unsuccessfully attempt to use it to comprehend information presented in other text genres. When introducing a schema for informational texts, it's important to show students how similar it is—that is, both have a beginning, a middle, and an end—and how different it is from a narrative text schema. When students develop schemas about the unique features of different text genres, they are able to anticipate the text's purpose (to entertain as opposed to informing or persuading) even before they begin reading the text. As they read, their brains will start to categorize the information in the neocortex, based on an existing schema. Anchor charts are one way to visually illustrate to students the schemas of literary versus informational texts.

Building a Procedural Schema

Let's look at procedural schemas in terms of math problems. When students try to solve math performance tasks (DOK 3) using the same simple procedures they used to solve math word problems (DOK 2), they will have little success. For example, a word problem (DOK 2) asks students to use the information in the table provided to figure out how much money was made selling lemonade. A problem-solving task (DOK 3) provides a table showing different ways to earn money and asks students to figure out the best way to earn enough money to buy a new bike before the sale ends in three days. Students need a more complex strategy for a more complex task that has more than one possible approach or solution. In my math problem-solving workshops, I start with a T-chart (see Figure 3.2) to compare the schema most teachers already know (solving a word problem) with the new schema I want to teach them (solving a math problem using performance tasks). I model how to collaboratively build the left side of the chart with participants as a teacher might do with students, then I elaborate on the differences between the two approaches, filling in the right side of the chart.

FIGURE 3.2
Comparing Procedural Schemas

Solving Math Word Problems I can . . .	Solving Math Problems Using Performance Tasks I can . . .
Read the problem for key words or phrases.	Read the problem for key words or phrases.
Determine what's being asked and identify the operation needed.	Determine what's being asked and think about how many different ways I could solve the problem: which strategies or steps I could use and any visuals, representations, or tools that might help.
	List related math terms or symbols and any operations or concepts that will help solve the problem and support my reasoning.
Perform the operation, check my calculations, and show my work. Label my answer (e.g., with appropriate units, objects).	Perform operations and create a representation (e.g., graph, diagram) to support my approach and solution.
	Check calculations and show my work.
[The teacher then looks at the student work and tries to discern the reasoning used.]	Explain in two or three sentences how my strategy (e.g., making a diagram, estimating, creating a number line, using objects, counting by fives), calculations, and representations support my solution. This is called reasoning. Make a mathematical connection to the real world, based on this problem.

Teachers can develop an *anchor chart* with students that shows how they might apply a given process using a sample problem (see Figure 3.3). The anchor chart could highlight each step with capital letters and a corresponding visual: UNDERSTAND (a visual of eyes reading); PLAN A STRATEGY (visuals of models and symbols for possible operations); and SHOW EVIDENCE (phrases telling what you did). Finally, teachers should annotate a sample problem.

FIGURE 3.3
Sample Anchor Chart

To further solidify the problem-solving procedure (schema), students can work through another performance task together, following the step-by-step protocol aligned with the schema.

Students can also use a rubric aligned with the schema to score and annotate sample solutions. Here are some schema-aligned scoring criteria for mathematics problem solving:

- *Strategy:* The student's approach was appropriate to the task and yields an accurate solution (DOK 2).
- *Reasoning:* The student explains how calculations, representation, and strategy support the solution (DOK 3).

- *Math communication:* The student accurately uses math terms and symbols (DOK 1).
- *Math representation:* The student supports the solution with a labeled diagram, graph, or table (DOK 2).
- *Connections:* The student makes and explains real-world math connections (DOK 2 or 3).

You can also use procedural schemas, such as a math problem-solving protocol or experimental design protocol, to guide peer feedback and self-reflection activities.

Building Schemas and the Actionable Assessment Cycle

Building a schema involves categorizing information, identifying relationships, constructing representations, and evaluating the effectiveness of the strategies practiced. For lesson planning purposes, the strategies included in this chapter work best during the earlier stages of the Actionable Assessment Cycle—before most students are ready to go deeper into the content with complex tasks. Once students have practiced the new strategies, they should be able to use them fluently and expand on them over time. You can also use many schema-building strategies as scaffolding to support language skills or executive function or to deepen knowledge.

Let's now look at how you can apply schema building to the first five stages of the Actionable Assessment Cycle.

Stage 1. Clarify learning targets.

To determine when or where building a schema might benefit your students, take a few minutes to consider the unifying concepts (declarative knowledge) and essential skills (procedural knowledge) for your content area. Enduring understandings typically include broadly stated concepts and skills that are at the heart of the discipline. For example, an enduring understanding in math might be, "Nature is filled with mathematical patterns." We sometimes refer to these as the *big ideas* of a discipline. This is *not* the same as listing all your standards or reviewing a smaller set of standards you've prioritized. Enduring understandings are insights gained over time, cutting across units of study and grade levels. We use them to develop essential questions for students to investigate and uncover deeper meaning. Briefly revisiting the enduring understandings for a unit of study can prime the pump for thinking about content-based patterns you might want to emphasize. Figure 3.4 illustrates the relationship among enduring understandings, essential questions, and schemas students might use to make meaning during learning.

FIGURE 3.4

Enduring Understandings, Essential Questions, and Sample Schemas

Topics/Content Areas	Enduring Understandings (also called *big ideas*)	Sample Essential Questions	Sample Schemas That Show Patterns or Relationships
Mathematics	Nature is filled with mathematical patterns.	Do some patterns help us predict future events or outcomes?	• Population or disease growth patterns • Statistical analyses
Science	All organisms have structures that help them survive.	How are structure and function related in living things?	• Structure–function relationships of plants and animals • Patterns of life cycles
Social Studies Fine Arts Graphic Arts	Art reflects the culture and history of people and society.	What can we learn about a society's culture or history from analyzing their art? Does history repeat itself in works of art or advertising?	• Purposes and use of color, space, design principles, symbolism in the fine arts
Language Arts	Writers use specific techniques to engage readers, viewers, and listeners.	What techniques do speech writers use to engage their audiences?	• Genre-specific structures • Literary devices and narrative techniques with distinct purposes

Stage 2. Embed short-cycle formative tasks into instruction.

Opportunities to deepen conceptual understanding help students connect ideas, explain relationships (for example, if/then, cause and effect, compare and contrast), and ask questions that reflect substantive understanding, such as, *What are the essential characteristics and structures of __[invertebrates]__?* The complexity of the schemas will vary depending on the subject area and scope of the unit of study. You can embed the following short-cycle strategies in almost any lesson to spark and personalize thinking.

Sketchnotes and Mind Maps. Sketchnoting can help students of any age connect to, organize, and retain complex information while listening, viewing, discussing ideas, or documenting thought processes and observations during an investigation. Taking notes using visual images, rather than words alone, enables the brain to use both hemispheres to make meaningful and personalized connections between stored prior knowledge and new information. Engaging the brain more fully also increases students' ability to remain focused. Sketchnoting (sometimes called *mind mapping*) is not the same as drawing a picture or making a detailed diagram. Learners don't have to be artists to be able to sketchnote.

Because this strategy is probably new to your students, take time to introduce and practice sketchnoting by modeling it while thinking aloud ("How could I show this with a quick doodle?" "Would an arrow here help?"). Then ask students to make quick doodles for others to guess the meaning of (for example, a person, an animal, a tree, or a house). Students might want to play a challenge game, making mystery "sentences" using only simple images for others to "read." You can also develop an icon database with students to use for different content areas (for example, light bulb = idea/invention; feet = travel; eye = examine; cloud = think).

Once students are comfortable with sketchnoting, provide a structural frame—such as a blank timeline, storyboard, or tic-tac-toe format with blank boxes—for them to visually capture ideas as they listen to or view a text. Teachers need to monitor pacing so that students have time to listen for a short time, stop to sketchnote, listen, and stop again to sketchnote. A 4th grade teacher from Colorado said that when he introduced a new social studies unit on African countries, he gave students a blank grid to capture their initial ideas about each country while he described a few interesting facts about each one. His students' sketchnotes were the starting point for summarizing what they heard and for later creating ABC books about Africa.

Paint the Parts. Ample research supports the use of color-coding to enhance memory and information retrieval. This strategy expands on a strategy I learned decades ago called the *painted essay*, which creates a color-coded visual model illustrating how informational texts organize information. (See "Related Resources" for a link to the Vermont Writing Collaborative and the original painted essay.)

When learning the basic parts of an essay, students begin by reading an essay together to locate each of its parts: the introduction, body paragraphs, and conclusion. After discussing the purpose of each part, students use watercolors to paint each part. They paint the introduction red because it grabs the reader's attention. They paint the first body paragraph yellow and the next blue to show that each paragraph elaborates on a different idea (highlighted by the paragraph's topic sentence). They paint the concluding paragraph green because it synthesizes ideas from the body of the essay (mixing yellow and blue makes green). Students can circle transitional words and phrases that connect body paragraphs to conclusions to indicate links on a chain connecting ideas. After analyzing and collaboratively painting an essay's schema, students can then create group and individual essays, "painting" them to reinforce the structural schemas of different genres of writing. Similarly, students can use highlighters, index cards, or sticky notes of different colors to break down schemas of more complex genres, such as the parts of an opinion or argument or the parts of an experimental design (hypothesis, variables, procedures, data tables, and conclusions).

Let's look at how we might color-code the "handy" brain model referred to in Chapter 1. We could paint the palm (limbic system) red because it can stop information from flowing to other parts of the brain. We could choose bright orange for the pinky fingers (occipital lobe) and bright yellow for the ring fingers (temporal lobe) because our senses bring in information that catches our attention. We could paint the middle fingers (parietal lobe) green, representing "Go," because movement and physical activities help process sensory information. Finally, we could choose purple for the pointer fingers and thumbs (neocortex), representing deeper critical and creative thinking processes.

Anchor Charts. Building anchor charts with students helps them visually reconstruct how the parts work together to create the whole. For example, anchor charts illustrating different text structures might define each structure with a visual icon (sequence = ladder; chronology = clock). Anchor charts created early in the learning cycle can reinforce new schemas, provide scaffolding, and be elaborated on throughout the school year.

Stage 3. Uncover thinking and document evidence of learning.

Picture Sorts for Visual Categorizing. Provide students with a group of related pictures (such as of a caterpillar, milkweed pod, chrysalis, and butterfly), or have them use a key word to search for related images. They can then sort the images to develop visual collages of a concept or big idea, such as, "All living things have life cycles," or to interpret and explain relationships among the parts. You can use technology tools, such as Google Draw, to locate images ahead of time, or you can codevelop concept collages with students and build content-specific vocabulary in any content area.

Find the Outlier. This strategy is a variation on picture sorts and visual categorizing. Include one image (or physical object, artifact, or vocabulary term) that doesn't belong in a group of images related to a concept or procedure. Students describe what does and doesn't belong, providing supporting reasoning. You can use this technique as a quick pre-assessment to spark small-group discussions or later in the unit as a formative probe. You could also give students a blank template, such as a storyboard or graphic organizer, and have them place various images in it to show how those ideas relate; they would also explain what didn't fit and why they left that item out. As a review activity, small groups can create "outlier challenges" for peers to solve. Expressing conceptual reasoning is the key to these activities.

Word Splash. Teachers can employ Word Splash for the schema-building retrieval practice of *interleaving* (Oakley et al., 2021). Interleaving can enhance procedural memory by mixing up different topics or forms of practice for deeper learning. In math, students might study for an exam using a variety of questions (for example, decide whether to use mean, mode, or median to solve) as opposed to practicing a single type of question (for example, calculate the mean using different numbers). An art teacher might present different artistic styles of famous painters or different genres of music with the intention of having students retrieve stored information about each part before making sense of it as a whole. A word splash presents several related vocabulary words and phrases randomly across the page (see Figure 3.5, which features words and phrases related to the term *revolution*). Some terms, but not all, are probably already familiar to students. A question box appears at the bottom of the page with a prompt requiring students to connect ideas.

FIGURE 3.5
Word Splash Visual

Word Splash for (topic) Revolution
inventions   **social**   American   Only some wars   **overthrow**   **government**
What do you know now about the meaning of revolution? Answer this question using some or all of these words and phrases to explain the connections among them.

Source: From *A Local Assessment Toolkit to Promote Deeper Learning* (p. 127), by K. Hess, 2018, Corwin. Adapted with permission.

As an informal pre-assessment, the teacher can use Word Splash to determine common misunderstandings; this helps determine which topics to preteach and which terms to focus on in readings, role plays, and class discussions. As students learn more about the topic, whether it's immigration, homeostasis, or revolutions, they can revisit earlier responses and self-assess their progress as they deepen their understanding. You can employ Jamboard for word splashes remotely, using one term per note card. Students can discuss, manipulate, and organize the information to collaboratively create two to three sentences using the vocabulary terms in the splash.

Graphic Organizers. Well-designed graphic organizers encourage students to prioritize and organize information conceptually using a visual format, tapping DOK 2–type thinking. You can use graphic organizers with sketchnoting and many other note-taking and discussion strategies. Arrows and headings in a graphic organizer help students consider how the information is connected, instead of asking them to simply fill in the boxes. For example, a graphic organizer for cause-and-effect is more helpful in guiding student thinking if an arrow points from the section for causes to the section for effects. Phrasing with the arrows helps clarify the differences, as seen in Figure 3.6.

FIGURE 3.6
Graphic Organizer for Scaffolding Concept Development

Causes These come first . . .	Leading to	One or More Effects . . . and these are the results.
Invention of electricity	→	• Led to inventions of household appliances • Made life easier for people who could afford appliances • People were now able to work in the evening
	→	
	→	

Pattern Folders. When I prepare to write an article or a book, I create both digital and hard-copy folders to help me organize my ideas. My folders have sticky notes to remind me of connections I want to make and include excerpts from articles I want to cite. My strategy is similar to one I saw in a lesson featured on the Teaching Channel, "Pattern Folders—A Literary Analysis Tool" (see "Related Resources"). Here, students gather evidence about a topic on index cards and organize that evidence by putting the cards in different pockets in a given pocket folder. Distributing the cards this way helps them see emergent patterns or themes and draw conclusions based on the evidence collected. As the students identify potential patterns during reading—political, say, or social—they label the different folders with these titles. Students can then sort and re-sort the index cards with their notes as they begin to see patterns and relationships with topics in each folder. Pattern folders are also an excellent scaffolding strategy for executive function to help students keep track of and categorize pieces of evidence from different sources (DOK 2) and support conclusions about themes (DOK 3).

Stages 4 and 5. Interpret evidence and frame feedback; determine next steps to advance learning.

Jigsaw the (Structural) Schema. Traditionally, the Jigsaw is a scaffolding strategy teachers use to divide up complex content; each member of a home team goes to a different group to discuss and become experts about specific content. Then they return to their home group to teach the content to team members, and together they integrate what they learned. In this iteration of the Jigsaw strategy, different groups of students study one aspect of a text—of an argumentative essay, for example. The teacher uses the Jigsaw structure not to divide up content for students to read and understand, but for students to examine different components of an argument so that they can build a schema about the genre of argument writing. While one group is identifying and analyzing rhetorical strategies used in the essay, another group might be discussing the clarity of the claim and counterclaim. A third group might be checking the accuracy and relevance of evidence used to support the claim or counterclaim. Every group has to read the entire text several times to determine how their part supports or interacts with the rest of the text. The Jigsaw activity encourages discussion and deeper thinking while students focus attention on how smaller parts relate to the whole. This strategy can begin with clear models and mentor texts and move to addressing more complex texts as students develop a deeper understanding of how to establish a logic chain with supporting data and evidence and how to use narrative and rhetorical strategies. Structural Jigsaws are also good preparation for peer conferencing, providing feedback to each student.

Collaborative Inquiry Planning (a Procedural Schema). This strategy requires students to use their prior knowledge about conducting investigations to plan *how* they will work together to complete a task. The planning tool (see Figure 3.7) lists common components of successful group investigation, such as clarifying their task, the skills and concepts they will use during the investigation, the specific resources they will need, the tasks and steps they will need to complete, how they will assign roles, and how they will assess the quality of their results. Teachers do not give students a plan. Students discuss and develop their own plans, which they then review with the teacher for approval before obtaining materials and beginning their work. This strategy gives students some autonomy in deciding how to transfer what they know about investigation to a new situation. It also sets the stage for peers to self-assess progress in meeting their group goal.

FIGURE 3.7
Collaborative Inquiry Planning Tool

Investigation Team: **Date:**
Goal: Describe the task or project in your own words.   We are trying to find out _____   _____   _____   _____
Concepts and skills we'll apply:
Our Plan for Investigating

Our Steps and Procedures What we will do.	Equipment and Resources What we will need.	Roles and Responsibilities Who will do each task.

Success criteria: How will we know if we're successful?
Submit your team plan for approval.   • **Needs more work:**   • **Approved—Ready to go!**

Source: From *A Local Assessment Toolkit to Promote Deeper Learning* (p. 81), by K. Hess, 2018, Corwin. Adapted with permission.

To Sum Up

Figure 3.8 summarizes how you might apply some of these actionable strategies during learning to deepen understanding and build schemas. You can use many of these multiple times in different content areas.

So far, we've looked at essential teacher move 1—asking probing questions—and essential teacher move 2—building schemas. Let's now turn to essential teacher move 3—considering strategic scaffolding—which we will address in the next chapter.

RELATED RESOURCES

- **Edutopia Videos**
  www.youtube.com/channel/UCdksaQxXH13BMeHo09MorBg

- *How to Sketchnote: A Step-by-Step Manual for Teachers and Students* by Sylvia Duckworth
  www.sylviaduckworth.com/how-to-sketchnote-a-step-by-step-manual/

- **"Jigsaws: A Strategy for Understanding Texts" (video)**
  https://learn.teachingchannel.com/video/jigsaw-method

- **Now Spark Creativity**
  www.nowsparkcreativity.com

- **"Pattern Folders—A Literary Analysis Tool" (video)**
  https://learn.teachingchannel.com/video/literary-analysis-tool

- **Sketchnotes: Suggested Strategies**
  https://knowledgequest.aasl.org/sketchnoting-in-the-library

- **Sketchnotes: Supporting Research**
  www.schrockguide.net/sketchnoting.html

- **"The Writing Recipe: Essay Structure for ELLs (video)**
  https://learn.teachingchannel.com/video/ell-essay-structure-lesson

- **Vermont Writing Collaborative**
  www.vermontwritingcollaborative.org/projects-and-resources

FIGURE 3.8

Actionable Strategies for Building Schemas

Actionable Assessment Cycle Stages	Strategies	Primary Purpose	Look Fors: Students build schemas when they . . .
1. Clarify learning targets.	Essential Questions and Driving Questions	Overarching unit questions determine potentially useful structural or procedural schemas for instruction.	Break down essential or driving questions into topics to investigate.
2. Embed short-cycle formative tasks into instruction.	Sketchnotes Mind Maps	Reinforce focus and listening skills; personalize connections during note taking.	Summarize or explain connections among key ideas (e.g., procedures, story lines, sequence of events, terms).
	Paint the Parts	Use color-coding to differentiate the parts from the whole.	Use physical, textual, or visual models to identify or apply schemas.
	Anchor Charts	Use color-coding, visual images, and key words to differentiate the parts from the whole or parts of a schema.	
3. Uncover thinking and document evidence of learning.	Picture and Word Sorts Find the Outlier	Categorizing, concept development, reasoning skills.	Use visual and textual sources to apply reasoning and describe conceptual understanding.
	Word Splash	Concept development; identify common misconceptions; retrieval practice (interleaving).	Make connections among concepts to demonstrate understanding.
	Graphic Organizers	Concept development, reasoning skills.	Identify patterns and explain connections.
	Pattern Folders	Concept development, reasoning skills.	Identify potential patterns or themes.
4. Interpret evidence and frame feedback. *and* 5. Determine next steps to advance learning.	Jigsaw the Schema	Concept development, peer teaching, reasoning skills.	Analyze a final product to ensure the parts support the overall quality of the finished product.
	Collaborative Inquiry Planning	Schema retrieval practice, peer goal setting, planning, reasoning skills.	Develop a plan to guide investigations.

4

Consider Strategic Scaffolding

In the 1930s, Soviet psychologist Lev Vygotsky developed the concept "zone of proximal development" or ZPD ... to test [students'] ability to solve problems both independently and with the help of a teacher. In 1976, Vygotsky's work was revived by researchers David Wood, Gail Ross, and Jerome Bruner, who coined the term "scaffolding."... [They] found that encouraging students to challenge themselves in grasping new concepts within their ZPD leads to success in learning.

—Rebekah Sager, "What Is Scaffolding in Education?"

I've often observed teachers using scaffolding without first considering the intended learning targets for the lesson and the reasons why particular students might struggle to achieve them. *Strategic scaffolding* can advance and deepen student engagement when we start by identifying the specific goal for using a strategy and which students will most likely benefit from that support. A scaffolding strategy intended to support executive functioning or language development, for example, may not be effective for deepening content knowledge and thinking. Educators should begin by asking themselves why they chose a given strategy, whether it matches their learning target, and whether it will optimize learning for their students.

But first, let's clarify the differences between scaffolding and differentiation.

Scaffolding or Differentiation?

Many educators—and even educational materials—confuse scaffolding with differentiation. However, they are actually quite different. An easy way to remember the difference is that scaffolding provides *steps* to support completing a task, whereas differentiation gives students *different choices* as to which tasks they will complete. When we differentiate instruction, students choose and work on different assignments. Teachers can create assignment options by differentiating the content (different texts, materials, situations, or topics), the processes used (engagement with the content or working alone or with others), or the products students develop as evidence of their learning. Teachers often use choice boards and assignment menus to describe the options available to students. (See more about this in Chapter 5.)

In contrast, scaffolding strategies enable each student to successfully access grade-level content, complete an assignment, and grow in confidence and independence as a learner. Although scaffolding is temporary, students can use many of the same strategies later on with more complex tasks or texts. Scaffolds are not only for struggling students; even high-performing adults break down complex tasks into smaller chunks and use models and peer feedback to improve their understanding. All learners benefit from the strategic use of scaffolding.

Scaffolding doesn't change the rigor of a task, but it can reduce the demands on a student's working memory during learning. For example, if the teacher reads aloud a complex text or presents it as a graphic novel, students don't need to use all their working memory to decode unfamiliar words to build basic comprehension. Instead, students might sketchnote while listening to capture key ideas that will help them explain a possible theme for the story, a process that is more complex than decoding. Although decoding skills are important, they're not the primary focus in this learning activity. Knowing what the learning targets are helps teachers determine which scaffolds are most appropriate for that lesson and for this or that student. In other words, the scaffolding activity is in students' zone of proximal development. Scaffolding ensures that the student's struggle will be productive.

Let's look at four ways to structure scaffolding:

- **Teacher and peer scaffolding.** Teachers can provide supports when introducing new concepts, tasks, or thinking strategies (for example, developing a mathematical argument) and then gradually remove them over time. Peers can read and discuss various texts, challenge one another's ideas, or collaboratively solve complex problems. Other examples of teacher-designed scaffolding include word walls, guided think-alouds, and recorded minilessons that students can view on demand.

- **Content scaffolding.** Teachers can introduce more basic versions of content or concepts before asking students to tackle more challenging ones. Scaffolding might involve using paired texts that are less complex or a short video that provides background knowledge. Teachers can use mentor texts that clearly illustrate a key teaching point—on flashbacks, say, or elaboration—to focus a minilesson. Literature in the form of graphic novels breaks text into smaller chunks with supporting visuals. (See "Related Resources" for a link to the Literal app, which enables students to read full unabridged novels in the form of text messages on their cell phones.)

- **Task scaffolding.** Teachers can break multistep, complex tasks into smaller steps. Students can practice basic skills in isolation (DOK 1), then apply those skills in routine tasks (DOK 2), then use them later in problem-based activities (DOK 3) with less complex content, and finally practice them with guidance before tackling more challenging tasks independently. Using technology tools, such as calculators or graphing software, is another way to minimize cognitive load during problem solving.

- **Materials scaffolding.** A number of materials support students in uncovering predictable patterns in texts or problem-solving contexts. These include nonprint texts (such as audiobooks, videos, or kinesthetic and interactive materials), graphic organizers, study guides, embedded visual cues (such as color-coding, visual icons, annotated exemplars, or hyperlinks), and chunked texts.

But Which Scaffolding to Use?

The choice may depend on *cognitive demand*, also called *cognitive load*, which describes the range of mental processing required to complete a given task within a given context or scenario. Think of scaffolding as a bridge that can either make content more accessible or make multistep tasks more manageable.

Determining the intended cognitive demand of an assignment requires more than simply identifying the verbs and nouns of the standards. Teachers must consider the reasoning and decision making required to complete a task successfully. For example, which thinking skills and depth of content knowledge do students need to check the reliability of sources, use supporting evidence, or design an investigation?

The key question for teachers is this: How can scaffolding help students show what they know by making content more accessible or by supporting the processing of content? Some scaffolding strategies can actually serve dual purposes. For example, many questioning strategies (such as Think-Pair-Share, Turn-and-Talk Frames, Picture Talks, and Question

Sequencing) and schema-building activities (such as Paint the Parts, Anchor Charts, Word Splash, Pattern Folders, and Jigsaw) also support and scaffold learning. (See Appendix B, "Teacher Tools," for a summary of scaffolding strategies by DOK levels.)

Why Use Scaffolding During Instruction?

Keeping the focus of learning on deeper understanding for *all* students means that teachers must be willing to shift their role as the person who delivers direct instruction to being more of a strategic learning coach. In turn, this will shift the role of students, who, instead of simply acquiring information, will be called on to produce and deepen knowledge.

When I work with schools to analyze and refine their instructional and assessment practices, we explore how administrators and instructional coaches can support both teachers and students in the classroom. They can best provide strategic support to students by

- Understanding how the brain works and how to optimize memory and learning.
- Clarifying learning targets and knowing what behaviors to look for that indicate cognitive engagement.
- Developing a repertoire of instructional and assessment approaches linked with indicators of rigor.
- Using ongoing formative assessment to understand the unique needs of students and adjust instruction to meet those needs.

Let's look at three reasons to scaffold during instruction.

Reason 1. To deepen content knowledge and connect to big ideas.

Equity begins with the belief that all students need to move beyond simply memorizing routines and acquiring surface knowledge—and that all students are capable of doing so. This especially applies to students with learning disabilities and multilingual students, who often receive low-level drill activities instead of more challenging instruction. Studies have shown that English learners need daily opportunities to use creative thinking, make sense of information and ideas, ask questions, and engage in research and inquiry (Commins, 2011; Gibbons, 2009). As Goudvis and colleagues (2012) noted, "Immersing students in a rich curriculum that values thinking and understanding over memorization and rote learning is the best way we know to encourage children to develop their identities as eager, curious learners—aware of the power of their own ideas, insights, and thinking" (p. v).

Many strategies used to deepen learning can flow out of activities designed to build language or support executive function. For example, developing an anchor chart with students on the steps (procedural schema) they need to solve a nonroutine mathematics task will encourage them to use the chart to trigger reminders of each step when solving new problems. Likewise, after clarifying the meaning of the academic language used in a learning target, such as "making an inference," a teacher might model a think-aloud using a multistep process for making inferences and then guide students to use a tool such as the one shown in Figure 4.1.

FIGURE 4.1
Active Reading Guide: Making Inferences and Analyzing Texts

Before you begin, identify your purpose: Why are you looking for text evidence? (Check any that apply):

_____ development of theme　　_____ character change over time　　_____ potential bias

_____ examples of author's craft/literary devices　　_____ other _____

1. As you read, note the page number and details (e.g., descriptions, what was said or done) of important **explicit** information that is clearly stated in the text.

2. "Read between the lines." What **implicit** information is suggested by each example of text evidence (e.g., what does it tell you about character motivations or creating a particular mood)?

3. When you have completed the reading, review your notes and **draw conclusions** about the text as a whole, based on the information you collected and analyzed.

Page Number	1. Relevant explicit information	2. What does the explicit information imply?

3. Conclusions
Using an analysis of text evidence related to your purpose (examine development of theme, identify potential bias, etc.) what conclusions can you make across the whole text?

Reason 2. To facilitate executive function and the application of skills and processes.

Students with poor executive function struggle with sustaining focus and engagement with lengthy texts and multistep tasks. Executive function also affects the ability to set and monitor goals and maintain a positive self-image as a learner. According to Wilson and Conyers (2015), "Students can and should be taught to develop their executive functioning as a path to self-directed learning and self-determined living" (para. 7).

In this chapter, scaffolding that promotes executive function focuses on the following skills:

- **Initiation:** The ability to begin a task or activity and independently generate ideas, responses, or problem-solving strategies (for example, clarifying "messy" objectives).
- **Working memory:** The capacity to hold information in mind for the purpose of sustaining engagement with a task (for example, chunking texts, sketchnoting).
- **Planning and organization:** The ability to manage current and future-oriented task demands (for example, collaborative inquiry planning).
- **Self-monitoring:** The ability to monitor one's own performance and to measure it against a standard (for example, conferencing, scrum boards).

Reason 3. To support language and vocabulary development.

Building vocabulary and using language are foundational to learning in all content areas. In the case of English language learners, one method for building vocabulary is to reinforce the language needed for learning in English language arts, mathematics, science, or social studies. For example, teachers can refer to the WIDA (2020) consortium's English language development standards (see "Related Resources") as they create learning targets and teach key academic language uses (explain, narrate, inform, argue) and communication modes (expressive) for demonstrating learning.

When planning instruction to support language development, keep the following in mind.

Language dimensions, structures, and models. When planning instruction, consider the three dimensions of language use within a sociocultural context (words/phrases, sentences, and discourse), beginning with *discourse*. As Lundgren and Willner (2012) note, "A discourse focus strengthens the interface of language and content learning and helps prepare students to engage in different communicative purposes—such as explaining how or why something works or retelling events in a personal story" (p. 1). Discourse itself has various dimensions, ranging from a broader focus on declarative statements and claims; to a narrower focus on sentence structures, such as using clauses to frame details and including pertinent examples; to an even narrower focus on word choice, such as using descriptive nouns, verbs, and adjectives.

Once teachers have targeted various language uses for instruction, they should consider which organizational structures and cohesive devices (such as developing schemas) and which grammatical structures and key vocabulary they need to teach. You can embed many of the techniques in this chapter in daily lessons to teach the various dimensions of language that English language learners need for learning and discourse.

Teachers can support language development using visuals and physical models to prompt prior knowledge. To emphasize importance or differences, they can use color-coding in anchor charts, sentence stems, or paragraph frames or to differentiate the place value of multidigit numbers. For example, when teaching essay writing, teachers could have students lay out different colored note cards—one card for the introduction at the top; several for body paragraphs below, each with a new subtopic (body paragraph 1, body paragraph 2, body paragraph 3); and one at the bottom for the conclusion—so that students visually see the flow of their ideas. Teachers might also structure purposeful discourse and model thinking aloud.

Preteaching vocabulary. Preteaching terms or phrases before teaching a lesson or reading a passage is often on a teacher's short list of vocabulary development strategies. However, we sometimes err on the side of introducing more words than most brains can handle at one time. When deciding what to preteach, ask yourself several questions:

1. Is the word, phrase, sentence structure, or organizational structure identified in grade-level cluster language expectations?
2. Is a particular word necessary for comprehension but *not* defined in the text or materials?
3. Is the word necessary for comprehension but *is* defined in the text or materials?
4. Is the word necessary for comprehension and is defined partially or implicitly in the text or materials?
5. Is the word not necessary for overall comprehension but perhaps is interesting?

You only need to preteach words that fall under the first two questions.

Margarita Calderón (2011) suggests a seven-step strategy you can implement daily for teaching vocabulary to multilingual learners. This works well for introducing everyday words that students might not know (tier 1 words) and academic words with potential multiple meanings (tier 2 words):

1. Show and say the word; students repeat or pronounce it three times.
2. Read the word in a sentence to show context.
3. Provide the dictionary definition.
4. Generate words familiar to students to paraphrase the word's meaning.
5. Highlight multiple meanings or a unique spelling of the word.
6. Use a Think-Pair-Share activity to practice using the word.
7. Assign peer reading, with students summarizing the material either orally or in writing.

Another quick strategy is simply to ask students to divide a learning journal page into four equal sections and write the new word in one section. As they read or view short chunks of the text, they stop to turn and talk with a partner, writing their own definition in a second section. In a third section, they draw a picture interpreting how the word is used in the text. After additional reading and after having engaged in large-group discussions to fine-tune definitions, students can add synonyms or illustrate different meanings of the word in the last section of the journal page.

Applying Strategic Scaffolding to the Actionable Assessment Cycle

Teachers can use the strategies described here to deepen knowledge, support language development, or facilitate executive function. Various strategies align particularly well with each of the stages of the Actionable Assessment Cycle, depending on your learning targets. Once students have practiced using these strategies, many will be able to use them independently as academic work becomes more complex.

Stage 1. Clarify learning targets.

Clarifying "Messy" Objectives. This strategy helps students break down unfamiliar academic language to build vocabulary and better understand assigned tasks. For example, teachers might write this lesson objective on the board: "I can write a narrative based on an image." They then draw a box around the word *narrative*, and the class discusses what a narrative is. They also write down synonyms familiar to students (*story*, *fairy tale*) near the word in a different color. Then they move to the word *image* and add words or draw pictures as reminders of what an image is. (See "Related Resources" for a link to the English Learner Portal website for a video modeling this strategy.)

Visual Orientation Cues. Many teachers with whom I worked during school shutdowns had concerns about engaging students right at the start of the lesson, especially their English language learners. At the Magnet School for Leadership and Innovation Through STEAM in New York City, a strategy that worked well for teachers in both remote and in-class learning was to create an *orientation screen* to begin the lesson. Rather than seeing a list of materials needed for a lesson, the students saw picture icons instead—of a notebook, ruler, or pencil, for example. A clock icon appeared, with the number two, which meant the students had two minutes to gather these materials and be ready to start. Teachers set a timer visible on the screen, which counted down the two minutes. When the buzzer rang, every student would hold up the requested materials to show they were ready to start. This might seem silly or obvious, but allowing extra time and using visual and auditory cues engaged the students. Many K–4 teachers also added a strategy called Sticker Face that a teacher had posted on YouTube. Instead of putting a sticker on a student's paper, the students tell their teacher where to put a sticker for an excellent response—on the teacher's face. Teachers typically used this strategy at the end of a lesson. As they made positive comments about each student's work, the teacher's face became covered with stickers. Both strategies promoted positive emotional engagement for students and teachers.

Thinking Verbs. Here, a consistent set of visual icons used across the school represents definitions for common academic words, such as *analyze* (which might be represented by a magnifying glass), *calculate* (which might be represented by a calculator), and so on. Everyone viewing the images, which teachers can embed in assignments and scoring guides, understands expectations. (See "Related Resources" for a link to the English Learner Portal website with information about thinking verbs.)

Stage 2. Embed short-cycle formative tasks into instruction.

Teaching Cognates. For multilingual students who have at least advanced beginner proficiency in their heritage languages, consider teaching cognates. According to Colorín Colorado (2007),

> Cognates are words in two languages that share a similar meaning, spelling, and pronunciation. While English may share very few cognates with a language like Chinese, 30–40% of all words in English have a related word in Spanish. For Spanish-speaking students, cognates are one bridge to learning the English language. Children can be taught to use cognates as early as preschool. As students move up the grade levels, they can be introduced to more sophisticated cognates, and to cognates that have multiple meanings in both languages, although some of those meanings may not overlap. (para. 1)

Paraphrase Passport. This strategy promotes active listening and speaking and builds language comprehension skills. Students can use this when they work in pairs or to make connections in larger-group discussions. When students want to add information or make a comment, they must first paraphrase what the last person just said ("What I think I heard you say is ____"). Then they can add to or extend the idea ("I think this is important because ____" or "Another reason might be ____"). Because students are bringing in prior knowledge and making connections using this strategy, it is likely to elicit DOK 1 or 2 thinking, encouraging near transfer.

Talk Moves. I first saw this idea in a Teaching Channel video, "Improving Participation with Talk Moves" (see "Related Resources"). Teaching students a few talk moves, such as sentence stems, reinforces how to contribute to a discussion in any content area. In the math lesson featured in the video, a 4th grade teacher has taught her students to use four different talk moves during class discussions. *Repeating* (DOK 1) keeps students engaged, focused, and ready to go deeper. *Adding on* (DOK 2) helps students make connections ("I'd like to add something new"). *Silent signal* is a hand signal that means, "I'm thinking what you're thinking." Of course, the only way to determine DOK levels for silent agreement is to prompt students to share their thinking (for example, "Can you provide a reason why you do/do not agree?"). The fourth talk move, *changing your mind when given new information*, asks students to explain how the evidence changed their thinking, a DOK 3–type talk move. (See "Related Resources" for an upper-grades example using more sophisticated talk moves, "Encouraging Academic Conversations with Talk Moves.")

Sentence Stems. Teachers can use sentence stems to scaffold—or jump-start—responses when students might not be sure how to put information together coherently. Depending on the stems used, this strategy can support developing language and vocabulary skills, trigger executive function, or deepen content knowledge. Sentence stems work well as turn-and-talk frames or for writing short journal entries. Figure 4.2 shows how sentence stems can serve different purposes.

Vocabulary Paint Chips. This strategy uses a physical model—paint chip strips from the hardware store that show darker to lighter shades of the same color—to visually clarify that words can have similar, but different meanings. To introduce this strategy, start by putting the word *cold* at the middle of the strip. Ask students what other words can mean different degrees of cold (such as *chilly, freezing, frigid,* or *icy*) and where they should place them on the strip to show that the meaning is getting stronger. *Freezing,* for example, would be colder or "stronger" than *chilly.* Above "cold," degrees of warm to hot could be listed. Students can develop word strips using a thesaurus to find synonyms for new vocabulary words.

FIGURE 4.2
Sentence Stems: Scaffolding for Different Purposes

Reinforcing Language and Vocabulary Skills	Supporting Executive Functioning	Deepening Learning
This is a fact _____, and this is an opinion _____.	An example that supports my idea or opinion is _____. This example shows _____.	I agree/disagree with this point about _____ because _____.
I solved this using _____. My first step was _____. My graph or diagram shows _____.	My investigation question is _____. I want to find out _____. I will use this tool _____ to measure and record _____.	This part _____ was interesting/confusing to me because _____.
When I put this noun _____ with this verb _____, I can make this sentence _____.	Today I observed _____, and now I wonder _____.	This problem _____ reminds me of _____ because _____.

Hint Cards. Providing students with a hint while they're working helps reduce the cognitive demand of the task and support information retrieval. Teachers can use both anchor charts and hint cards to do so. In a Teaching Channel video, "Hint Cards," a teacher anticipates what her students might struggle with and creates several hint cards that students can use if they get stuck while solving the problems (see "Related Resources"). Cards include a reminder of the procedural steps to use and an annotated problem example. Other hint cards might define key terms or provide a formula, rule, or structure for organizing information; offer an internet link; or list questions to think about when solving a given problem. Although the learning tasks shown in the video focus on near transfer (DOK 2), the Hint Cards strategy can work effectively in many different content areas with more complex tasks. Figure 4.3 illustrates ways to provide scaffolding hints without changing the overall rigor of the task.

Read-Draw-Write and **Read-Draw-Do.** Read-Draw-Write is a prewriting strategy where students read or view a short literary or informational text passage. Next, they make a sketch to show what the passage was about. Finally, they use a paragraph frame or graphic organizer to write a response to a given prompt. Read-Draw-Do works well for problem solving in math, but teachers can use it in other content areas as well. Students interpret information presented in the problem by first drawing and labeling the problem situation (for example, a mom cut a pie into eight equal pieces; four pieces were eaten). Then students solve the problem.

FIGURE 4.3

Sample "Hints" to Trigger Recall and Organize Thinking

Definitions, Rules, Formulas, Hyperlinks (DOK 1)	A mean is one way to express the average.
Graphic Organizers for Data (DOK 2)	List chores / Monday earnings / Tuesday earnings / Friday earnings / Total earnings
Graphic Organizers Color-Coded for Parts of a Scientific Explanation (DOK 3)	Claim → Evidence, Evidence, Evidence → Reasoning
Procedural Steps (DOK 2)	**Read** and understand the problem. **Plan** a strategy and carry it out. **Draw and label** a diagram. **Use evidence** to support your solution.
Sentence Stems for Responses (DOK 1 and 2)	What I just read/observed makes me think about _____. I think this idea is similar to _____ because _____.

Stage 3. Uncover thinking and document evidence of learning.

Paragraph Frames. Just as sentence stems provide support and structure for speaking and listening, paragraph frames do the same for putting sentences together into a coherent paragraph. One way to create a paragraph frame is to analyze a mentor text with students, taking a paragraph apart to create a generic frame for that text structure, be it description, procedural sequence, chronology, or cause and effect. For example, students might analyze a well-constructed paragraph for compare and contrast to create a frame with blanks for the items they're comparing (see Figure 4.4). Then they use the frame to write new paragraphs comparing two other things. Paragraph frames can emphasize the use of transitional words and phrases and signal words unique to different text structures (for example, time order signal words might include *first, next, later, soon after,* and *finally*). Signal words in the sample paragraph frame shown in Figure 4.4 are italicized.

FIGURE 4.4
Sample Paragraph Frame for Compare/Contrast

A _____ and a _____ are *similar,* but also *different* in several ways. One way they are *alike* is _____. Another way they are the *same* is _____. And *they both* _____. There are also *differences between them.* For example, _____, whereas the other _____. Another *contrast between them* is _____. My conclusion is that they are more (different/similar) because _____.

Chunking Print and Nonprint Texts. One way to keep students engaged with lengthy, grade-level, print or nonprint texts and build stamina at the same time is to break the material into meaningful chunks. For video clips and podcasts, a chunk must be long enough to express a key idea or describe an event. For informational texts, a chunk might be the information appearing under each subheading. Students must answer a given question after each chunk—such as, *What do you think will happen next and why?* or *What new information was just revealed?*—with the most complex question coming at the end of the text. That way, students are able to process smaller pieces of information along the way before having to answer an overarching question at the end, such as, *What is the author really trying to say?* or *Why did the authors write this?*

Chunking texts using teachers' questions is a precursor to teaching students how to annotate texts. Students might begin by underlining a key word, phrase, or sentence in that chunk; paraphrase what that phrase or sentence means; and write a question or reaction to what that chunk is saying (for example, *Did something surprise or shock you? Is there something you disagree with or wonder about?*). When students are learning how to annotate, using sentence stems initially provides support until they get the hang of it. Annotation also supports the important skill of summarizing after reading.

Partner Collaborations. This is so obvious that teachers might overlook it as a scaffolding strategy. Working in the smallest of groups encourages full engagement, individual accountability, and flexible thinking through focused dialogue. For example, when using paired texts, each partner has a different role related to a larger task. Each student locates information from a different text before collaboratively integrating or contrasting the ideas presented. Although students are still expected to integrate ideas from multiple sources, this strategy lessens the cognitive load. Partners can incorporate other strategies to keep them focused, such as *selective highlighting* (using different colors for key ideas) or *structured note taking* (discussing how best to fill in a graphic organizer, such as TBEAR, described at the end of this section). Pairs can also sort pictures or visuals representing main ideas and supporting details to create a visual concept map.

Building a Mathematical Argument. I often suggest the following strategy for supporting mathematical problem solving. Partners divide their paper in half lengthwise. On the left, the students work through each step to solve the problem. On the right, they explain why they did each step or how that helped (for example, "My diagram shows how the candy bar was divided; I labeled each fractional part"). Teachers at all grade levels have found this strategy to be effective because it breaks down *how* the student got to the solution and slows down thinking so that they can explain *why* they did each step. Figure 4.5 shows what a worksheet might look like.

"Daily 10" Playlist. The effect of background knowledge on reading comprehension and schema building cannot be overstated. To use this strategy, teachers create a playlist of short print and nonprint resources on a topic (for example, photos, political cartoons, articles, or websites related to a social studies or science unit). For about 10 minutes a day, individual students or groups of students choose one resource to read or listen to, and they take a few notes. Class discussions and journal writing can connect students' growing background knowledge to the ongoing unit of study.

Daily note taking can include using a five-box grid for adding a sketchnote each day, employing sentence frames for daily journal entries, or organizing notes synthesized from whole-class discussions on chart paper. In virtual classrooms, teachers can use a collaborative slide deck to capture note facts. Readworks (www.readworks.org) curates literary and informational text sets on many K–12 topics, which you can draw from to create playlists for classrooms.

FIGURE 4.5
Template for Building a Mathematical Argument

The Problem:	
Complete each step you took to solve this problem. *What* did you do?	Below, write a few words explaining *why* you did this step or how it helped.
1.	
2.	
3.	
4.	
5.	
Use your explanations for each step to develop a mathematical argument. Explain *why* your strategy, your representations, and your calculations all support your solution.	

Wonder of the Day. An alternative to creating a "Daily 10" playlist is to identify a key word related to the focus of your unit to use with the website Wonderopolis (see "Related Resources"). Students generate and search questions they wonder about—such as, *Do glaciers still exist?*—using the key word in question. The website then populates with related short texts and videos, often with key vocabulary words highlighted, to scaffold reading. After reading or viewing the material, students summarize what they learned from different articles so that peers can compare and share new facts on the topic.

TBEAR. I've used the graphic organizer TBEAR for more than a decade at many grade levels with great success. (See "Related Resources" for a link to download the TBEAR template.) TBEAR effortlessly scaffolds students to move from DOK 1 to DOK 2, 3, or 4, and the acronym makes it easy to remember what each part stands for:

T: Write a **T**opic sentence/**T**hesis statement or claim (DOK 1), or define a vocabulary **T**erm or concept.

B: **B**riefly summarize the text as a **B**ridge to evidence (DOK 2), or paraphrase the meaning in your own words.

E: Locate text **E**vidence or **E**xamples (DOK 2), or provide both examples and nonexamples when defining domain-specific terms.

A: **A**nalyze every example or each piece of text evidence; **A**dd more information to elaborate or to explain why the evidence supports the thesis/claim (DOK 3).

R: State something to **R**emember (DOK 1 or 2) or a **R**eflection that may go beyond DOK 3 to DOK 4 (for example, text-to-world connections, personal connections, connections to other sources).

To introduce how to use TBEAR to break down and analyze text evidence, I incorporate a text familiar to most students. For younger students, this might be a fairy tale. This approach works especially well for students with limited language proficiency skills. Working as a whole class or with a partner, students can use TBEAR as a guide to locate text evidence and prepare for class discussions or writing. Middle school teachers in Hawaii with whom I worked had students create anchor charts (with visuals or examples and nonexamples) for key math vocabulary words after analyzing them using TBEAR.

Stages 4 and 5. Interpret evidence and frame feedback; determine next steps to advance learning.

Carousel Feedback. This strategy is a variation on carousel brainstorming and is illustrated in a lesson on the Teaching Channel, where a geometry teacher heterogeneously groups students and has them rotate from one multistep problem to another. Student groups read the problem at their table and begin to solve it on chart paper. After a few minutes and before they have finished, time is called and the groups rotate to a new problem. There, they read the problem from the last group and check that group's work so far. After discussing what they see in their peers' work, they decide if the last group was or wasn't correct up to that point. They use a new color marker to either continue working on that problem if it is correct so far or make corrections if they see a mistake. If they have to correct the problem, they write a side note justifying what was wrong and why and how they corrected it. Time is called again, and groups rotate to a third problem, using the same checking and justifying process as before. In the last round of rotations, groups develop a mathematical justification supporting the solution based on the calculations, diagrams, and notes of the other teams.

Teachers can use Carousel Feedback rotations with many different content areas. Students can build on the ideas of others through progressive group writing or troubleshoot what's wrong with a vehicle or graphic design based on the data presented. Strategies such as these promote deeper discussions and collaborative reasoning even when assignments begin with a basic task, such as solving a routine mathematics problem or developing a summary or story line for a text.

Emojis. I observed this scaffolding strategy in a high school English class several years ago. Students were reading *Macbeth*. Actually, the teacher was reading *Macbeth* aloud, and pairs of students were following along and interpreting character interactions. Then they used text evidence to create character emojis depicting what each character was feeling in the scene. This strategy lessens the reading load while focusing attention on interpreting the text and supporting explanations with close reading and specific text evidence.

EKG. Similar to character emojis, the EKG strategy, like the electrocardiogram (EKG) technology it is named for, visually represents rising and falling emotions, interactions, or conflicts brought on by events or changing situations. On an EKG chart, students note the rising or falling actions and annotate the reasons behind those actions based on text evidence. I've also seen students use EKGs to depict what happens when two chemicals meet or to plot events leading up to a historical event.

Stage 6. Use performance tasks to assess transfer and deepen learning.

Jigsaw the Content. In this approach, students in the home group are split up to work as expert groups, with each group analyzing a different resource. They then return to their home groups to teach team members the content and integrate ideas drawn from different sources. Students often use a graphic organizer or guiding questions to structure their note taking. Teachers can divide a single article into short chunks, with each expert group reading and discussing a different chunk before they teach or summarize ideas for peers. When I taught middle school, I used Jigsaw with my 7th graders by assigning different chapters to each expert group. Using the first chapter, I modeled how to make a timeline of events and identify and define new vocabulary in the chapter. That was the structure each group used to present their chapters to peers.

Minilessons and Video Guides. Teachers can record a minilesson (under six minutes) for students to view as often as needed (before, during, or after class). As with print texts, you can chunk your recorded minilessons to keep each part short, maintaining learner focus. Many screencasting tools are available for creating such videos (Farah, 2020). High school science teacher Alison Stone (2022) prerecords lab video guides that include detailed instructions for students to read beforehand to maximize learning time when they do their biology lab. Stone has used Edpuzzle (https://edpuzzle.com) to create a video and quiz and Microsoft Sway (https://sway.office.com/my) to create a lab manual.

Recorded minilessons and video guides have several advantages. They provide auditory, visual, and written supports to activate students' memory, reducing cognitive load. They offer flexible access and scaffolding for students who need it or extension activities for students ready to move ahead. They free up time during class for the teacher to check in with groups and ask or answer deeper questions. A high school math teacher told me that when she flipped her instructional time by assigning her minilesson on the "basics" as homework, she had more class time for in-depth problem solving. Students can create their own video guides and minilessons to demonstrate their learning or teach peers. (See Chapter 5 for guidance on planning minilessons.)

Scrum Boards. A scrum board is a strategy used in business and industry to track team progress on complex projects (LaVogue, 2020). Scrum boards give students control in managing their work and timelines while visually enabling teachers to supervise the progress of multiple teams. You can configure scrum boards in many ways. The scrum board shown in Figure 4.6 has several columns, with space for each team to track their work. LaVogue suggests that because the boards are public, it's preferable to list team names rather than individual student names.

Teams begin by listing on sticky notes all the tasks they need to complete to finish a multistep project. Teachers can review the tasks if they wish. All tasks start under the "To Do" section. Once a team begins to work on a task, they move that card to the "Doing" column. Before task cards can move to the "Done" column, members of another team will analyze the work and provide feedback in the "Feedback" column. Once the peer group initials the task card as complete, the card is placed in the "Done" column. At a glance, teachers can get a quick idea of what teams are working on and who might need support.

FIGURE 4.6
Scrum Board Example

Team Names	TO DO Tasks we need to do to complete our project	DOING NOW Tasks we are now doing	PEER FEEDBACK Tasks that peers are reviewing	DONE Tasks that we have now completed after peer feedback and our revisions
	☐ ☐	☐	☐	☐ ☐
	☐	☐	☐	☐

To Sum Up

Figure 4.7 summarizes several ways you might apply the strategies described in this chapter to scaffold deeper understanding. You can use many of these strategies in a variety of content areas.

In the chapter that follows, we'll look at essential teacher move 4—designing complex tasks for all students.

RELATED RESOURCES

- **"Carousel Activity: Rotating Through Geometry Stations" (video)**
  https://learn.teachingchannel.com/video/carousel-activity-math-lesson

- **"Clarifying 'Messy' Objectives" (video)**
  www.englishlearnerportal.com/blog-messy-objectives

- **"Color-Coding: The Differentiation Strategy You Never Knew You Needed" by Allyson Caudill**
  www.weareteachers.com/color-coding-classroom

- **Designing Socratic Seminars to Ensure That All Students Can Participate**
  www.spencerauthor.com/socratic-seminars

- **"Encouraging Academic Conversations with Talk Moves" (video)**
  www.edutopia.org/video/encouraging-academic-conversations-talk-moves

- **"Hint Cards" (video)**
  https://learn.teachingchannel.com/video/hint-cards

- **"Improving Participation with Talk Moves" (video)**
  https://learn.teachingchannel.com/video/student-participation-strategy

- **Literal (minimal monthly per-student charge to subscribe)**
  http://read.literalapp.com

- **TBEAR Template**
  www.karin-hess.com/_files/ugd/5e86bd_20f99d299eba462194e40d7cf26b2ffa.pdf

- **"Thinking Verbs: Improve Academic Language with Thinking Verbs" (video)**
  www.englishlearnerportal.com/shop

- **Understanding Language, Supporting ELLs in Math**
  https://ul.stanford.edu/resource/supporting-ELLs-mathematics

- **Universal Design for Learning/UDL (CAST)**
  www.cast.org/impact/universal-design-for-learning-udl

- **WIDA Consortium's English Language Development Standards**
  https://wida.wisc.edu/teach/standards/eld

- **Wonderopolis**
  www.wonderopolis.org

FIGURE 4.7
Actionable Strategies for Strategic Scaffolding

Actionable Assessment Cycle Stages	Strategies	Primary Purpose	Look Fors: Students use supports to . . .
1. Clarify learning targets.	Clarifying "Messy" Objectives	Review and clarify academic language in lesson learning targets.	• Clarify task expectations.
	Visual Orientation Cues Sticker Face	Provide visual supports when introducing materials or procedures needed for the lesson.	
Actionable Assessment Cycle Stages	**Strategies**	**Primary Purpose**	**Look Fors: Students use supports to . . .**
2. Embed short-cycle formative tasks into instruction.	Teaching Cognates	Teach words in English that are similar in meaning, spelling, or pronunciation to words in another language.	• Use language skills in daily speaking, listening, and writing activities.
	Paraphrase Passport Talk Moves	Practice speaking and listening skills using verbal cues.	
	Sentence Stems	Build vocabulary; reinforce and connect ideas.	
	Vocabulary Paint Chips	Build vocabulary based on shades of meaning.	• Identify synonyms.
	Hint Cards Anchor Charts	Support retrieval of stored information during a problem-solving activity.	• Complete multistep tasks.
	Read-Draw-Write Read-Draw-Do	Interpret information read, viewed, or heard by drawing the problem and then solving or writing about it.	
3. Uncover thinking and document evidence of learning.	Paragraph Frames	Analyze mentor texts to create frames for writing types of paragraphs.	• Use language skills in writing activities.
	Chunking Texts Annotating Texts	Use embedded questions after text chunks to slow down and process the entire text; support summarizing and elaborating on key ideas.	• Identify key ideas and summarize content of print and nonprint texts. • Sustain engagement with longer texts.
	Partner Collaborations Structured Note Taking	Pairs discuss and analyze information presented.	• Identify key ideas and summarize content of print and nonprint texts. • Sustain engagement with longer texts.

(continued)

FIGURE 4.7
Actionable Strategies for Strategic Scaffolding (*continued*)

3. Uncover thinking and document evidence of learning. (*continued*)	Building a Mathematical Argument	Solve a complex math problem, explaining *why* each step was helpful.	• Complete multistep tasks and explain their reasoning for the steps used.
	"Daily 10" Playlist Wonder of the Day	Build background knowledge and note-taking skills.	• Build background knowledge on a topic and apply that knowledge to new learning activities.
	TBEAR	Promote concept development and reasoning skills.	• Scaffold language development at the discourse level. • Promote executive function and content processing.
4. Interpret evidence and frame feedback. *and* 5. Determine next steps to advance learning.	Carousel Feedback	Use reasoning skills during problem solving; peer feedback/critique.	• Break down and complete multistep tasks. • Apply reasoning skills.
	Emojis EKG	Visual representations for depicting interpretations of texts or events.	• Identify key ideas of print and nonprint texts. • Analyze and use text evidence.
6. Use performance tasks to assess transfer and deepen learning.	Jigsaw the Content	Groups become experts on different resources and teach peers.	• Complete multistep tasks. • Identify key ideas and summarize content of print and nonprint texts.
	Video Guides Recorded Minilessons	Guides students through a complex activity or provides targeted instruction.	• Complete multistep tasks.
	Scrum Boards	Team management tool tracks progress; peer feedback and critique.	• Monitor multiple tasks during the project. • Provide peer feedback using specific criteria.

5

Design Complex Tasks

What makes the driver's performance assessment valid is that it directly exhibits the actual skills needed, as they are used in the real world. The assessment does not need to be secret to be a useful test, since the driver must work to acquire and display the necessary skills in order to pass... a robust performance assessment evaluates the way in which knowledge and skills are mastered, combined, and used in practice.

—Roneeta Guha, Tony Wagner, Linda Darling-Hammond, Terri Taylor, and Diane Curtis,
The Promise of Performance Assessments

Years ago, I heard Howard Gardner make a comment that has stayed with me all this time: "Every complex task in life is a project, and we rarely—if ever—do them alone." The point I think he was making is that we can tackle much more complex, performance-based tasks when we work on them with others than we can if we work on them alone, especially when we're first learning *how* to do those tasks. Since that time, cognitive science has supported his point (Hess et al., 2014; Pellegrino & Hilton, 2012).

In this chapter, we'll tackle how to design complex tasks. But first, let me say that not all projects and all performance-based assessments (PBAs) are created equal.

The Evolution of Performance-Based Assessments

My performance-based assessment practices have evolved since my first years of teaching when I was using something I now call "PBA 1.0." At that time, I created fun, engaging, and memorable projects related to the social studies or science units I was teaching. My students and I enjoyed the projects because they broke the monotony of memorizing facts and routines and often integrated content from different subject areas. And although I knew some learning was taking place, I never really measured or documented it beyond engagement and task completion. Thinking back on that earlier time, I mostly designed my projects as engaging instructional activities.

When states began to adopt academic standards, I saw great value in creating rich assessment tasks that could engage my students in learning at deeper levels while tapping multiple standards. With colleagues, I used backward design to develop and validate performance tasks that showed that students were meeting the standards in different content areas. I call this period "PBA 2.0." This approach was a significant improvement over the loosely designed projects that were missed opportunities to determine what students had actually learned.

Many educators currently implement variations of PBA 2.0, which aligns assessments with content standards and student engagement with deeper learning. Annotated student work samples illustrate the quality of the work and show whether the student has met the success criteria. Teachers form professional learning communities to build a common understanding of what "good enough" looks like in student work across classrooms and schools. Validation and calibration protocols adopted systemwide become ongoing embedded professional development opportunities for educators. The result of fully implementing PBA 2.0 is a high-quality assessment system with equitable learning opportunities for every student. We could just continue to use PBA 2.0 as our model for assessing deeper learning. The strategies in this book promote instructional practices that support this approach.

For students to truly transfer learning and construct knowledge that is personally meaningful, however, they need to take an active role in designing and assessing their own learning. This brings me to PBA 3.0—designing assessment opportunities with student choice and voice as design features, especially for the more complex tasks. PBA 3.0 is similar to the earlier standards-based PBAs, but it incorporates academic content with the application of personal skills and dispositions, such as collaboration, critical and creative thinking, and self-direction (see Figure 5.1).

What High-Quality PBAs Look Like

Performance-based learning and assessment activities require students to *do* something and can encompass a range of possibilities, from short-cycle and teacher-guided performance tasks to inquiry-based investigations and senior capstone projects. PBAs demonstrate evidence of proficiency by creating authentic products of learning, such as designing a website, participating in a debate, or producing art. All performance-based tasks integrate and apply multiple skills, concepts, and strategies, whether it's learning to drive a car or composing a five-paragraph essay. Asking students to solve a mathematics problem using one strategy and then to use another approach to prove that the solution is correct demonstrates that the student has acquired and applied several basic strategies in mathematics and made conceptual connections when using them. Tasks such as these demonstrate *near transfer*— applying skills and concepts in the way they were taught. A beginning driver uses near transfer when learning how to apply the brakes while driving. More complex situations— such as braking on icy roads or in heavy rain—require more complex or nuanced solutions.

FIGURE 5.1

The Evolution of Performance-Based Assessment (PBA) Design

Assessment Design and Use	PBA 1.0	PBA 2.0	PBA 3.0
Description	Curriculum-related Teacher-designed projects, role-plays, and group or individual problem-solving activities	Curriculum-embedded, often with real-world connections Teacher-designed projects, performance tasks, and problem-based tasks aligned to academic standards or course requirements Uses student work samples to describe quality Systematic attention to academic standards, DOK level, and valid scoring rubrics	Curriculum-embedded or curriculum-extended, with real-world applications that are relevant to students' communities, cultures, and identities Teacher-guided or student-driven problem-based, inquiry-based, and project-based learning designed to transfer knowledge of academic content and employ personal skills and dispositions Uses student work samples to describe quality and student voice Systematic attention to academic standards, personalized learning, DOK level, and valid scoring protocols
Assessment Focus	Participation and engagement	Focuses on final products and demonstration of learning that meets grade-level academic standards	Focuses on both processes and products; demonstration of learning that meets grade-level academic standards and incorporates self-reflection on personal learning
Grading and Reporting	Either not graded or pass/fail grades show completion	Contributes to grade or standards-based grading in a content area	Contributes to a student's body of evidence or portfolio in demonstrating competency in both academic and interpersonal and intrapersonal skills

Complex performance assessments not only apply multiple skills, concepts, and strategies, but also provide opportunities for disciplined inquiry and critical and creative thinking. This is *far transfer*—applying what you know in ways you might not have been explicitly taught. To use a sports analogy, far transfer is playing the game using new combinations of acquired skills in unfamiliar situations. Teachers can also design complex tasks to elicit evidence of students' ability to apply interpersonal skills (collaboration, leadership) and intrapersonal skills (self-direction, self-reflection, goal setting) in developing a final product or performance. The crucial difference between PBA 2.0 and PBA 3.0 tasks is that the latter show evidence of far transfer in the final products of learning, as well as in the processes used to develop those products, which both teachers and students evaluate.

Let's look at seven common characteristics of these high-quality performance-based assessments. The first four focus on deep, authentic learning; the last three push students out of their comfort zones.

1. PBAs have open-ended contexts. Prompts or situations posed to students are open-ended and guided by essential or driving questions. Students are expected to use multiple approaches, tools, and resources. Solutions don't require a single correct solution path, and students must justify the path they chose with supporting evidence and reasoning. Success criteria reflect how authentic performances are evaluated for quality in the real world. For example, teachers would use the same criteria that videographers use to evaluate the quality of a student's video product. Problem solving in an auto shop class simulates what happens in the real world: Students must diagnose a problem, develop a plan to correct it, build the budget, communicate with the car owner, and complete the repair successfully.

2. PBAs productively challenge students. Open-ended essential questions cause students to grapple with concepts, test different approaches, stretch their thinking, and explore different solutions and constraints to arrive at a solution. They may need to test, get feedback, and redesign their solution. Perseverance and learning from mistakes are honored. Exploring a topic such as social justice challenges students to reflect on what they value and on how equitable solutions can positively affect others.

3. PBAs uncover thinking. Products and performances require students to engage in substantive reasoning related to concepts and theories and to make connections with enduring understandings and big ideas of a discipline. Generating questions, propositions, alternative strategies, and representations are integral to completing the task. Visuals, such as diagrams and graphs, show how the learner has made connections or interpreted findings. Students state their reasoning as part of a solution or in support of their conclusions.

4. PBAs promote authentic doing and sharing. Products and performances reflect real-world skills and dispositions. For example, science investigations apply schemas that scientists use to test claims of commercial products and share findings with the manufacturer, an authentic audience. Teachers need to consider how to help learners connect their products and solutions with audiences beyond the classroom.

5. PBAs that "stretch" thinking integrate academic knowledge, personal skills, and student input. When students collaborate to design and conduct a science investigation, they must document evidence of how effectively they used their science knowledge *and* how effectively they worked together. Peer critiques and self-reflection are integral to the process. Students make decisions about how or where they will work, the materials they will use, the questions they will investigate, and what their final product of learning will look like. (To guide students in planning an investigation, you might review the collaborative inquiry planning process described in Chapter 3.)

6. PBAs that "stretch" thinking require far transfer. Products and performances embed opportunities to apply prior knowledge of multiple academic concepts and skills in novel, real-world contexts. The processes that students use—deciding which skills and concepts to apply and what they learned from both trial and error and feedback—result in a learning stretch.

7. PBAs that "stretch" thinking spark reflective and metacognitive thinking. Unlike traditional tests that ask for recall and near transfer of skills and concepts, performance assessments require students to reflect on what they have done in the past, self-monitor how well what they're doing is working right now, and articulate what they learned and how they have extended their own knowledge. Self-reflection is intentional in the task or project design; it's not an afterthought. (Chapter 6 provides strategies to guide self- and peer reflections.)

Task Complexity: A Matter of Content or Engagement, or Both?

The answer to that question is "It depends." Educators and test developers frequently ask me why some assessment tasks or test items seem more challenging for students than others, even though the DOK levels are the same. The fact is, the DOK level (cognitive engagement) is only one aspect of task complexity. Summarizing a series of events in a picture book and summarizing key events in a novel are both at DOK 2. Readers have to locate, interpret, and organize the information to complete the task. However, the picture book can be less complex content to interpret than the novel.

So one continuum of complexity is the content. Another continuum refers to the task requirements or *engagement* with the content. Figure 5.2 shows four possible combinations of task–content complexity, all of which might be part of a well-planned unit of study.

FIGURE 5.2
Four Ways to Describe Task Complexity

Less Complex Content	Cognitive Engagement	More Complex Content
Type B Tasks **PBAs** Less complex content + More complex tasks (DOK 3–4)	DOK 4 DOK 3	**Type D Tasks** **PBAs** More complex content + More complex tasks (DOK 3–4)
Type A Tasks Less complex content + Less complex tasks (DOK 1–2)	DOK 2 DOK 1	**Type C Tasks** More complex content + Less complex tasks (DOK 1–2)

Let's look at the four types of tasks highlighted in the figure:

Type A tasks apply DOK 1 or 2 engagement to less complex content, concepts, or texts. Teachers might use them to introduce new content or check for understanding. Students often use Type A tasks to practice academic or personal skills with less complex content until they master the skills in question. Type A tasks include word problems in math and fill-in-the-blank, text-based questions. They're not performance-based assessments, but they are important for laying the groundwork for problem solving in all content areas.

Type B tasks might use the same content as Type A tasks, but they focus on more complex questions, such as, *What is a theme of this story?* (DOK 3) or *What universal themes are illustrated in the two stories we've already read?* (DOK 4). Supporting productive struggle with Type B tasks is about helping students engage more deeply with the content. Type B tasks are excellent for introducing more complex strategies for critical analysis—such as annotating texts or completing multistep problems—using familiar content or concepts. To that end, I often recommend that teachers introduce problem solving in mathematics using math content from an earlier grade or earlier unit of study to initially lessen cognitive demand on working memory. Once students demonstrate that they can use multiple strategies, representations, and math operations with less complex math concepts, they're ready for more complex content. The focus of Type B performance tasks is on solving, analyzing, creating, and using reasoning, not on mastering new concepts. These tasks include constructed-response questions requiring supporting evidence and PBAs with accessible content.

Type C tasks apply less complex DOK 1 or 2 thinking to more complex content, concepts, or texts. Supporting the productive struggle with Type C tasks is not about engagement as much as about helping students access and comprehend the content. Scaffolding strategies, such as chunking the text or providing a diagram or an embedded glossary, can make complex content more accessible. As with Type A tasks, Type C tasks are *not* performance-based assessments. They include word problems with complex math procedures, and they ask students to explain concepts or relationships, such as cause and effect or compare and contrast.

Type D tasks are the most complex combination, applying DOK 3 or 4 complex thinking to complex content, concepts, or texts. Sometimes teachers jump to using Type D performance tasks without any strategic scaffolding or before students have mastered the strategies with less complex content. Both approaches usually end in frustration for students and teachers. Before increasing content complexity with Type D tasks, try using Type B performance tasks with less content complexity, such as pairing a less complex text to provide background knowledge before introducing a second, more complex text. Planning several PBAs of increasing complexity from Type B tasks to Type D tasks forms that inner loop of the Actionable Assessment Cycle, giving students time and multiple opportunities to move their learning to deeper levels. Use strategic scaffolding as a bridge to either facilitate the engagement with content or unlock the complexity of content when introducing the most complex PBAs. This will ensure that every student has a greater opportunity to learn.

Questions to Consider as You Begin

Locating an existing task and tweaking it to meet your needs is a good first step to designing your own performance tasks, especially if you're just getting started. When I introduce my task and rubric design tools to teachers, we use them to collaboratively analyze existing tasks to see if we can locate each of the seven characteristics of high-quality PBAs. Don't be surprised to find that many PBAs are not designed to assess transfer of both academics and personal skills and dispositions. However, you can upgrade many readily available PBA 2.0 tasks to 3.0 by adding or strengthening opportunities for student input, voice, and self-reflection.

Before developing new tasks and scoring rubrics or determining what the final products will be, start by answering five key questions to frame your thinking as to the scope and intended depth of learning. As you read the questions, try to answer them using an existing performance task as a reference point.

1. **Validity:** *What (content + processes + personal dispositions) will be transferred during learning and will be assessed?* Many performance tasks ask students to apply personal skills, but they never actually assess them. If students are to set and monitor goals or work collaboratively, you need to plan how to collect evidence of those skills. Perhaps teams will use a collaboration rubric to self-assess or individuals will use journal entries to self-reflect at the end of a project.

2. **Alignment:** *How does this task align with local competencies or academic standards?* Competencies can include both academics and broader crosscutting skills, such as critical and creative thinking. Focusing on a small number of competencies or standards usually results in better alignment and a more manageable process of collecting evidence to document learning.

3. **Authentic context:** *Within what real-world context and format—a case study, a design problem, an investigation, or a simulation—will students solve a problem or investigate an essential or driving question?* This design feature includes two important points: Use real-world contexts and pose a broad essential or driving question to make learning relevant, open-ended, and intriguing.

4. **Student input:** *How will PBAs reflect the cultural diversity of learners? Will students have choices regarding the content, approach, or resources to use, and how they will share what they've learned?* This feature reinforces the importance of shifting roles from teacher-directed to student-driven learning. Leave some parts of the task design open for student input and decision making. If students are to create a specific product (for example, a short video), let them choose the topic.

5. **Opportunity to learn:** *Will all students have an opportunity to develop knowledge that they can transfer to a new situation or problem by engaging in this task? Is this task embedded in an instructional unit, or is it an opportunity to extend student thinking about an instructional unit?* Just as in a softball tournament, before expecting students to transfer skills, concepts, and dispositions, you must first teach and reinforce those skills through practice drills, scrimmages, and feedback—before they play the game.

Eight Steps to Designing Performance-Based Assessments

Let's now walk through how you can design effective performance-based assessments. The three-part process involves brainstorming ideas for task purpose and scope; putting the task description together; and creating directions, clarifying success criteria, and developing scoring rubrics.

Part 1. Brainstorming Ideas for Task Purpose and Scope

Step 1. Identify what you want the assessment to measure. Use the criteria shown in Figure 5.3—skills and processes, form, accuracy, transfer/construction of knowledge, and effect/impact on self and others—to generate the dispositions and thinking strategies you plan to assess. You don't need to include all criterion types in the final scoring rubric, but you should at least consider them during this phase of the planning. Only the last two criteria—transfer and effect on self and others—will actually assess far transfer of skills, concepts, or dispositions, so be sure to include one of them. The underlined criteria in Figure 5.3 are from my work with teachers in New Hampshire and the Chicago Public Schools developing performance-based assessments on the topic of social justice.

Step 2. Identify one or more authentic contexts for applying these skills, concepts, and dispositions in the assessment. Consider how real-world professionals—such as artists, historians, writers, scientists, health professionals, and educators—employ these skills and concepts. For example, as researchers, students must gather, organize, and analyze information using surveys, interviews, and research documents. In a science investigation, students might conduct field studies or labs. Group problem-solving activities might include engineering design tasks, dance routines, or mathematical modeling.

Step 3. Identify appropriate formats for how students will apply their knowledge, skills, and dispositions. These might include comparing case studies or recommending solutions after case analyses; role-playing scenarios, such as mock trials or interpretive dance; developing a product, such as an infographic, a podcast, or a documentary; community service projects or awareness campaigns; self-reflection journals; or peer critiques.

Step 4. Identify which choices, input, or decisions students will make. Give students a range of choices—about the topic or focus of the task, whether they want to work in a group or individually, which tools and resources they want to use, what timeline they require, and what product they want to create and for which audience.

FIGURE 5.3

Developing Performance-Based Assessments (PBAs): Criteria and Options

Criterion Types	Related Questions	Possibilities for PBAs **Topic:** *Social Justice*
Skills and Processes (DOK 1 or 2 for more complex tasks)	**Will the student use specific processes or tools?** These may include procedures for <u>research</u> or a science investigation, data collection tools and analysis, <u>validating the credibility of sources</u>, and use of technology or software.	*Teams choose a local or global perspective to focus their research, find data or documented examples of social "injustice," and validate sources using a checklist provided (and modeled earlier).*
Form (DOK 1)	**Will the student be required to apply specific formats or rules?** These may include the correct <u>citation</u> format, organization of a lab report, required camera shots, <u>editing</u> grammar and usage, and meeting deadlines.	*Students will use or cite multiple resources and apply the appropriate format for each team's product choice. This might require direct instruction and tutorials.*
Accuracy: Content and Concepts (DOK 1 or 2)	**What content knowledge must the student accurately apply?** These may include essential domain-specific terms, <u>concepts</u>, theories, symbols, and representations.	*The concept of social justice is key to this investigation. Students will codevelop understanding with their team and refine that understanding with research and discussion.*
Transfer: Interpretations and Construction of Knowledge (DOK 3 or 4)	**How will the student go beyond developing an appropriate product?** How will the student gain new insights, raise new questions related to the topic, or make connections to big ideas? How does this link to the <u>essential question</u>?	*Students will generate several related essential questions and choose one to guide their investigation.*
Effect (Impact) on Self and Others (DOK 3 or 4)	**How will the final product achieve its intended purpose?** How will the student solve a complex problem, inform or change perspectives of self or the audience, synthesize information to create a useful product or an entertaining performance, or justify a call to action and make a difference? How does this link to the <u>essential question</u>?	*Student journal entries will guide self-reflections related to the essential question.* *Teams will use a collaboration rubric.* *The final product will have an explicit message and make new connections.* *Perhaps students will have peer conferences mid-project to give and receive feedback.*

Source: From *A Local Assessment Toolkit to Promote Deeper Learning*, by K. Hess, 2018, Corwin. Adapted with permission.

Part 2. Putting the Task Description Together

Step 5. Describe the task. This chapter describes several PBA models: problem-based tasks, project-based learning, inquiry-based investigations, Global Challenge, and Genius Hour, to name a few. Your professional learning community teams may want to explore several models and use one of them as a template for customizing local PBAs.

Figure 5.4 shows my STARS framework for describing structure and areas of potential student choice in a given task. Each letter of STARS describes a different component of the PBA: the **S**cenario (or **S**ituation), the **T**asks, the **A**udience, potential **R**oles and **R**esources available, and the **S**elf-Assessment **S**uccess criteria. As you can see in the figure, success criteria include three components: content (major concepts, principles, or theories to demonstrate understanding and connect to big ideas and driving/essential questions); processes and thinking strategies (such as research, data analysis, creative problem solving, and design thinking); and products that show evidence of what the student learned. The question marks in the figure indicate areas of possible student input or choice.

Many products of PBAs include students giving oral presentations or writing essays, articles, or arguments, all of which are important skills to develop. However, students can demonstrate their learning in many other ways. For example, when I taught middle school, I required my students to use a different format each time they gave a book report. They quickly moved beyond doing posters and dioramas to creating dramatic presentations of crucial scenes and role-plays of interviews with characters, all of which were far more interesting for the audience and the presenters. When I work with career and technical schools, I often suggest having the students develop short tutorial videos to teach something they've learned, troubleshoot a flawed design or solution, or pitch a new design like a Shark Tank entrepreneur.

One way to introduce students to new ways of sharing their learning is to teach the class one new format, such as how to create a podcast. Students could begin by listening to a few published student podcasts and analyzing them using structured note taking. They could then choose a topic for their podcast, develop a script, and record and edit the podcast as a group. Although they won't be experts after their first try, they will have an idea of how to develop their own podcasts so that it becomes a viable choice for them in the future. Because TED Talks, video tutorials, and minilessons are similar to podcasts, a lesson later in the year might involve creating four "how to" stations: how to create a podcast, how to create a TED Talk, how to create a video tutorial, and how to teach a minilesson. Over time, students will develop confidence in trying new ways to share their learning.

FIGURE 5.4
Flexible Task Design with Student Input Using STARS

S Scenario Examples	T Tasks	A Authentic Audience	R Roles and Resources	S Success Criteria for Peer or Self-Assessment		
Describe a situation or real-world context.	*In this task or investigation, you will . . .*	*Identify peers, experts, or community members (local or global).*	*Identify roles, perspectives, and resources.*	*Content, concepts, connections to big ideas*	*Thinking processes (DOK levels)*	*Product(s) of learning*
Plan an event or a class trip.	Determine how best to spend or earn a given amount of money.	Convince the class your plan is the best plan.	?	?	Decide how to research ideas. Create a spreadsheet.	A business plan with data and timeline A debate
Create a design challenge.	Build or create a better way to _____.	?	?	?	Plan and design. Collect and analyze data.	A prototype that has been tested and refined
Tackle a "messy" problem in the news (e.g., a judge who lied under oath).	Determine whether the oath or guidelines for judges should be changed.	?	?	What is in the oath a judge takes? Are there penalties for lying?	Research points of view, consequences, and past cases.	A role play A public service announcement
Target a global challenge.	Choose one global issue: hunger, water, climate, health, etc.	?	?	?	Begin your research with a key word search.	A call to action; what do you want readers/ listeners to do?
Solve a multi-step problem.	Redesign a floor plan with the following criteria: _____. Develop a thematic banquet menu.	?	?	?	?	A budget and design that support the proposal
Create an alternative solution or model.	Choose an environmental problem to study.	?	Identify competing perspectives	Content specific to one of three student choices	Analyze case studies and related data.	?

S Scenario Examples	T Tasks	A Authentic Audience	R Roles and Resources	S Success Criteria for Peer or Self-Assessment	
Analyze a perspective on a topic of interest.	?	?	?	?	Annotate multiple texts on a topic.	?
Hold a Wonder Day. Conduct an inquiry-based investigation (IBI). Do a Genius Hour.	Investigate something you wonder about. Here is a chance to learn more.	?	Internet Experts Primary and secondary sources Art, lab, or construction materials/tools	?	Research and gather information (through interviewing field studies, etc.).	?

Source: From *The Rigor by Design Playbook: The What, the Why, and the How* (p. 18), by K. Hess, 2021, Educational Research in Action. Reprinted with permission.

Complex tasks require more complex products! Let's look at some products of learning that you might not be as familiar with.

- **Developing a Case Study.** Case studies are an excellent way to introduce complex information for students to analyze, especially in social studies and science, technology, engineering, and mathematics (STEM) classes. Students can also create case studies by taking an exemplar case study apart—to understand the schema of case studies—and then using that schema to build their own cases. They can present their case studies as written products or documentaries, or they might use media and visuals with voiceover narration.

- **Exhibitions and 5-Minute Film Festivals.** These are exhibition-type presentations, where peers rotate through stations, viewing student films that are each five minutes long or less, and write a quick reaction for the producers using various sentence starters: "The most interesting thing to me was _____." "I think _____ was effective because _____." "The theme was clearly illustrated by _____." "This made me think/ question _____."

- **Podcasting.** Students at any grade level can create podcasts to share their learning. Monica Brady-Myerov (2019) suggests using five steps to teach students how to develop a podcast: Students (1) listen to high-quality podcasts published for students to analyze what makes a podcast good; (2) plan what they want to say by researching the topic and drafting a script; (3) collaborate in the writing, recording, and editing; (4) seek ongoing feedback as they develop the script and final presentation; and (5) present their work to an authentic audience.

- **Thematic Food Trucks.** This simple and adaptable product organizes ideas around a theme using the visual of a food truck van. Culinary arts teachers can ask students to design a food truck theme, complete with menu and advertising. A social studies teacher might ask students to create a food truck representing what people ate during a given historical time period. Students need to provide their rationales (DOK 3) for each food item they include on the menu. Teachers can hold a "food festival" for peer critiques.

- **Performance Poetry.** Similar to digital storytelling, performance poetry is a powerful way for students to share their ideas with passion and special effects (such as voice modulation, props, gesture, and music). Students might start by watching a skilled orator deliver a poem, such as Amanda Gorman's recitation of her poem "The Hill We Climb" at the 2021 inauguration of President Biden. Discuss how the delivery enhances the meaning of poems from different cultures and time periods. Students might do a quick internet search to locate poems written to be delivered to a live audience and practice how they might perform one of them for peers. The class can even select the same poem for groups to perform; they can compete with one another in a poetry slam to rate the best delivery. A performance-based assessment can feature a poem that students have composed or one they've selected that captures the essence of what they have learned.

- **Blackout Poetry.** Students select or are given a short informational text on a topic. Using a black marker, they block out most words, leaving only the most descriptive phrases that share what the topic is about. They then combine those words and phrases to create a poem.

- **Shark Tank Proposal.** Most people are familiar with the TV program *Shark Tank*, where entrepreneurs try to sell an idea to get funding for a new product. Presenters must prepare an engaging overview and be ready for any question the "sharks" (business representatives) ask after listening to the pitch. This is a fun way to share final PBL products. Search "Shark Tank episodes with kids" for short videos of how students pitch ideas to sell products they've designed. For example, two boys proposed an edible add-on to an ice cream cone to catch the inevitable drips and drops.

For a more extensive listing of complex products that demonstrate learning, see Figure 5.5.

FIGURE 5.5
Authentic Products That Demonstrate Learning

• Action plan	• Food truck or kiosk based on theme	• Podcast
• Advertisement/commercial	• Game: board game, digital game, timed challenge game	• Political cartoon
• Annotated timeline		• Position paper
• Awareness campaign, public challenge	• Graphic design	• Prototype testing, product development
• Blog	• Graphic novel	• Public service announcement
• Blueprint, building models	• Infographic, poster	• Research study
• Book, film, music review	• Interactive map, display	• Science investigation
• Brochure, pamphlet	• Journal: reflective, digital, interactive	• Sculpture
• Business plan	• Letter to my future self, people of the world, authors, inventors, historians	• Self-reflection
• Comic strip		• *Shark Tank* proposal
• Critique: literary, scientific	• Memoirs, six-word memoir	• Simulation
• Data collection (interview, survey, focus groups, etc.)	• Minilesson, tutorial	• Storyboard, treatment
• Debate	• Model, scale model, 3-D model	• TED Talk, speech
• Develop a case study	• One-pager	• Trailers: book, amazing facts
• Develop (multimedia) argument	• Op-ed/opinion piece	• Travelogue, travel guide
• Digital storytelling	• Oral history	• Troubleshoot faulty designs
• Documentary	• Painting, printmaking	• Video: museum guide, how-to tutorial, minilesson
• Dramatic performance	• Performance poetry, blackout poetry	• Web page, website
• Exhibition, museum display	• Photo essay	• Write/troubleshoot computer code
• Field study		
• Five-minute film festivals		

Part 3. Creating Directions, Clarifying Success Criteria, and Developing Scoring Rubrics

Step 6. Develop an overview of the PBA with directions and general teacher instructions. The overview clarifies, among other things, the standards/competencies to assess, the enduring understandings and essential or driving questions, and the student prompt and general teacher directions. Figure 5.6 provides a template for developing an overview.

Step 7. Finalize success criteria. Review the student prompt to ensure that the criteria in the scoring rubrics clearly align with assessing the intended content, the processes used, and the final products created to demonstrate learning. You will often need more than one scoring rubric—one to assess academics and others for peer or self-assessments. Figure 5.7 illustrates a rubric that assesses collaboration skills; each rubric criterion is paired with a focus question written in student-friendly language.

FIGURE 5.6
Developing a Performance-Based Assessment (PBA) Overview

Project or Assessment Task Title: _____

Content Area: _____ Grade Level(s): _____

Unit of Study/Course: _____

Competencies/Standards Transferred and Assessed

- Academic Content: _____
- Interpersonal Skills: _____
- Intrapersonal Skills: _____

Enduring Understanding(s)/Big Idea(s):

_____

_____

Essential or Driving Question(s):

_____

_____

Student Prompt

Use STARS components (Situation + Task + Audience + Roles and Resources + Success Criteria) and student-friendly language. Clarify the choices or decisions students must make (e.g., which collaboration options to use, which texts to consider, which product to focus on, which questions to guide the research).

Describe Student's Role/Decisions/Engagement/Input into Task Expectations or Task Design

- Choice/decisions to be made *during* the assessment: topic, text, approach, materials, and so on.
- Opportunity for personal voice/perspective: _____
- Group collaboration/roles (*prior to* or *during* the assessment): _____
- Student input into task design or presentation/product format: _____
- Self-assessment, reflection, peer feedback: _____

General Teacher Directions

Task Description and Purpose: (How will this PBA help students transfer prior learning?)
This task requires students to apply _____ in order to _____.

Resources Needed: _____

Prerequisite Knowledge and Skills (to transfer): _____

Estimated Time Needed: _____

Grouping Strategies? _____

Suggested Use of the Assessment: Formative _____; Interim (midyear or mid-unit) _____; Summative _____

Additional Accommodations Allowed (e.g., use of audiobooks for a task requiring literary analysis; a recorded presentation as opposed to presenting before a live audience):

_____

_____

Success Criteria ("I can" statements that serve as learning targets and identify assessment evidence)

- **Content:** (I can . . . analyze the impact of techniques used by authors to convey a message.)
- **Processes:** (I can . . . evaluate the accuracy and credibility of sources.)
- **Products:** (I can develop a _____ to share what I've learned.)

Rubrics or Scoring Guides to Be Used for This Performance-Based Assessment or Project:

- Content knowledge, skills/processes, knowledge production, effect/impact
- Specific product formatting (e.g., visual, auditory)
- Peer assessment or peer critique
- Self-assessment or self-reflection

Source: From *A Local Assessment Toolkit to Promote Deeper Learning*, by K. Hess, 2018, Corwin. Adapted with permission.

Although this alignment check may seem obvious, many times the scoring criteria for complex tasks are not flexible enough to allow students to use alternate approaches or develop products using different formats. A rubric that assesses planning processes, content knowledge, and impact is suitable for a variety of final products; however, in some cases, you may want to use rubrics that specify which technical aspects to assess in, say, a podcast, an infographic, or a video tutorial. It's worth the time to develop rubrics for different product formats that you can use multiple times throughout the school year. Check to see if colleagues in the fields of graphic arts, visual arts, video production, and photography already have rubrics for these types of products.

Step 8. Develop a scoring guide or rubric. A well-written rubric provides direction to both teachers and students as to what to do next to advance the learning. You may eventually end up creating a teacher version with additional task-specific scoring notes and a student-friendly version for self- or peer assessment. (Chapter 6 includes examples of student scoring guides.)

When developed collaboratively with your professional learning community, scoring rubrics reflect shared schoolwide understandings of academic expectations; moreover, this process vastly improves both the quality and use of the rubrics. You can also codevelop rubrics with your students by showing final product exemplars or student work samples, guiding a discussion to derive criteria (such as, *What makes this an engaging video or useful diagram?*) and performance indicators based on the examples. (See the Rubric Quality Checklist in "Related Resources" under Hess Assessment Development Tools.)

Let's now look at a checklist for creating a high-quality rubric:

- **Opt for four performance levels rather than three.** When there are three choices, scorers tend to choose the middle option.

FIGURE 5.7
Focus Questions for Collaboration Rubric Criteria

Rubric Criterion	Focus Question
Reflecting on my role in a group	**Self-Awareness and Personal Responsibility** How am I building on my strengths, interests, and experiences when planning group tasks and working on my part?
Equitably and respectfully sharing ideas	**Communicating** Do I contribute my ideas clearly, listen respectfully, and encourage the participation of all group members?
Working through group differences or personal challenges	**Decision Making and Problem Solving** How do I show that I value others' perspectives and am willing to work with others to resolve conflicts among members, as well as my personal challenges?
Individual and group effort toward quality	**Contributing and Supporting** Do I contribute to group expectations by providing feedback on the work and ideas of others, completing my tasks, and assessing the quality of our results?
Evaluating group processes	**Monitoring and Adapting** How do the members of my group evaluate our progress and determine when and how we should modify our approach to benefit the group?

Source: From "Collaboration Rubrics (Grades K–2; Grades 3–5; Grades 6–8; Grades 9–12)," *Toolkits & Resources*, by BEST for the Future, 2022. https://best-future.org/resources/. Adapted with permission.

- **Use descriptive language.** Too many rubrics include vague, subjective, judgmental, or negative words (such as *often, rarely, poor, nice, messy, impressive*). If you find that the labels on a diagram are "inadequate," describe *why* they are inadequate so that the scoring is more reliable (for example, "Your labeling is inaccurate" or "Your labeling is incomplete"). Rather than say "insightful statement," which is subjective, describe what makes a statement insightful.

- **Focus on quality, not quantity.** The difference between performance levels should not simply be a matter of one more example, citation, or quote. More is not always better. Emphasize quality first. Quantity descriptors are most useful when identifying the number of task parts completed.

- **Keep wording stated in the positive for all performance levels.** Describe what you see, not what's missing (for example, "One of the three sections is complete," as opposed to "Two parts are not completed"). Begin with descriptors at the proficient level, explicitly describing the knowledge, skills, and performance expected. Next, describe scoring criteria for levels below proficient that don't include all elements; consider what the student might complete first, such as drafting a plan and collecting data (as opposed to analyzing data collected at an upper performance level).

- **Describe excellence, not perfection.** Often the best performance descriptions for advanced performance don't include a long list of things to incorporate into the final product. A better approach for describing advanced performance is this: "In addition to meeting all criteria for proficient, at least two or more indicators are also evident."

- **Describe a progression of observable indicators,** moving from less to more complex across performance levels. Consider including basic/foundational skills at lower performance levels (such as, "Identify at least two research sources") and move to more complex tasks and transfer of skills at proficient and advanced levels.

- **Be kid-friendly,** especially if you use headings for performance levels. For example, students say they prefer labels such as "Getting Started" or "Novice" over "Below Basic" or "Unacceptable," which are negative. After all, we've all been a novice at everything we've ever learned how to do.

- **Minimize the number of performance indicators for each rubric criterion.** All too often, rubrics list too many indicators to realistically evaluate. Try to prioritize the most important indicator. I call this *the chocolate chip cookie taste test*—if taste (impact) is a more important quality of the cookie than the number of chips, then focus on evaluating taste and perhaps weighting scores for that criterion.

Once the draft rubric is complete, review content, process, and impact criteria to ensure they apply to a variety of performances and products. When scoring criteria are flexible enough to assess multiple artifacts of student work, rather than only one specific product, students can demonstrate their knowledge and skills in a variety of ways, showing progress over time. Criteria and performance indicators that are "task neutral" help teachers to equitably meet the diverse learning needs of students, who may produce different products of learning, and to interpret assessment data meaningfully. You can use additional form-specific rubrics to evaluate different types of authentic products.

Figure 5.8 depicts a collaboration rubric that I developed that adheres to the guidelines for creating a high-quality rubric. (See "Related Resources" for BEST Toolkit and K–12 collaboration rubrics.) The shaded rows indicate criteria for self- and peer assessment.

FIGURE 5.8

New Hampshire Learning Initiative Collaboration Rubric for Grades 6–8

Collaboration Focus Questions	Extending I can also . . .	Applying I can also . . .	Developing I can also . . .	Emerging I can . . .
COMMUNICATING Do I contribute my ideas clearly, listen respectfully, and encourage the participation of all group members?	Contribute well-supported ideas and validate each team member's contributions with positive reinforcement and constructive feedback.	Work with my group to pose questions, seek feedback, and analyze different perspectives to modify a position or an idea.	Justify my point of view with supporting evidence and pose questions or give feedback to others to clarify their points of view (with guidance).	Share and elaborate on my perspectives and encourage others to share their perspectives during group dialogue (with prompting).
DECISION MAKING AND PROBLEM SOLVING How do I show that I value the perspectives of others and am willing to work with others to resolve conflicts among members, as well as my personal challenges?	Work with my group to evaluate possible trade-offs and merits of each idea and find a way to resolve conflicts that honors each member's contributions.	Work with my group to build consensus when determining tasks and roles needed to achieve group goals, based on each person's strengths or interests.	Use my understanding of differing perspectives and approaches to develop shared group goals, roles, and tasks.	Follow a process provided by the teacher to advocate for my ideas, consider the ideas of others, and work toward group consensus.
CONTRIBUTING AND SUPPORTING Do I contribute to group expectations by providing feedback on the work and ideas of others, completing my tasks, and assessing the quality of our results?	Analyze alternative approaches that could increase my personal learning or advance the overall quality of my group's performance.	Support my group by working to complete individual and group tasks and evaluating the effectiveness of our approach or quality of our final product.	Affirm the efforts and ideas of others and suggest ways to use them to advance group expectations and planning.	Explain how my contributions could help meet expectations for completing my group's work.
Self-Assessment SELF-AWARENESS AND PERSONAL RESPONSIBILITY How am I building on my strengths, interests, and experiences when planning group tasks and working on my part?	Describe how I contributed my strengths and overcame challenges to improve the quality of my group's final product.	Work with my group to set group goals, analyze possible approaches to accomplish tasks, and assign individual roles that maximize group potential.	Show a commitment to group goals and adjust my responsibilities to ensure that my contributions help my group meet success criteria for quality work (with guidance).	Draw on past experiences when working with my group to establish norms for group processes and guide my contributions to group tasks (with guidance).
Peer Assessment MONITORING AND ADAPTING How do the members of my group evaluate our progress and determine when and how we should modify our approach to benefit the group?	Work with my group to reflect on group progress and adapt norms, roles, or strategies to optimize the collective group effort and advance the overall quality of my group's performance.	Work with my group to analyze challenges, identify the need for different strategies, and adjust our approach to meet individual or group needs.	Contribute ideas and build on suggestions from others to make possible individual or group course corrections (with guidance).	Monitor my progress in completing tasks and work through challenges with help from others.

Source: From "Collaboration Rubrics (Grades K–2; Grades 3–5; Grades 6–8; Grades 9–12)," *Toolkits & Resources*, by BEST for the Future, 2022. https://best-future.org/resources/. Adapted with permission.

Aligning Performance Tasks with the Actionable Assessment Cycle

Take a moment to consider the progression of tasks students will complete during a unit of study. The unit or project probably begins with Type A tasks. These are like practice drills for a sports team. Use familiar content or concepts when introducing more complex strategies. Type B tasks are like scrimmages, putting skills and concepts together with initial guidance and support. If you want students to engage in more complex PBAs that emphasize transfer (the player actually playing the game), students need practice with scrimmages that foster deeper thinking. This is what the "inner loop" of the Actionable Assessment Cycle means: Teachers use feedback and scaffolding with multiple PBAs of increasing complexity to advance learning.

Let's look at how performance tasks align with the six stages of my Actionable Assessment Cycle.

Stage 1. Clarify learning targets.

Essential or driving questions frame units of study, leading to inquiry-based investigations using complex PBAs. Plan how several tasks of increasing complexity will deepen learning within a unit of study.

Stage 2. Embed short-cycle formative tasks into instruction.

"Reading" Visuals. Using visuals (photographs, symbols, illustrations, flowcharts) that require minimal or no reading is an effective way to introduce a new topic or provide background knowledge. Present students with the visual and ask for first impressions, observations, and questions. Pairs of students then share those impressions with each other and decide what they might already know (or not know) about the topic. Next, introduce a related visual; students can begin to make connections and generate new conjectures to investigate. Layer learning with each successive visual; for example, you might show students photographs depicting different time periods or video clips depicting before-and-after scenes.

Ask Three Sources. Many teachers have used the rule "ask three before me" to encourage students to seek help from other resources (peers, texts, hint cards) before coming to the teacher for help. When students start to frame ideas for an investigation, suggest several reliable websites for them to consult or tutorials on creating different products (infographic, web page, storyboard, and so on). You can do this as a mini-Jigsaw in groups of three, each student locating information from a different source and reporting back to the team on what information was useful or relevant.

Graffiti Boards. A graffiti board is a visual and somewhat random way to begin to gather ideas in response to an open-ended question, a data set, a text, artifacts, photos, or current events. For in-person lessons, use sticky notes posted on a chart paper to display initial ideas or comments; Google Docs, Jamboard, Padlet, Flipgrid, or VoiceThread work well for virtual environments. Once ideas are posted, ask students to consider the following, in either large- or small-group discussion: *What do you notice in these ideas? Can we group them in some way? Are there any common themes? Where are there disagreements?*

You can also use graffiti boards to pre-assess prior knowledge or generate investigable questions or possible solutions before problem solving begins. The Facing History and Ourselves website (see "Related Resources") provides visuals and details of how to use graffiti boards with both in-class and remote learning.

Stage 3. Uncover thinking and document evidence of learning.

Anticipation Guides. Anticipation guides are excellent discussion starters and self- and peer assessment tools that require supporting evidence for opinions in any subject area. Students consider one to five statements related to the topic at the start of a lesson or unit of study. Some statements can be true/false, whereas others should require interpretation or drawing conclusions. Students mark each statement with either "agree" or "disagree." After reading, discussing, observing, or solving a problem, students revisit their earlier responses and decide if their opinions have changed, providing reasoning and evidence for their final responses.

Stations. As early as the 1970s, elementary teachers have used stations to manage small-group work, with students moving from one station to another about every 15 to 20 minutes. Today, teachers at all grade levels use stations in both remote and in-person settings. Teachers can use stations as "rotations," with each group moving station to station, completing the same activity at each one, or as "differentiation" activities either chosen by students based on interest or assigned by the teacher to specific students. Students complete different tasks during station differentiation. The total number of stations is flexible, determined by the number of students you want working in each group.

Station activities can include direct teaching or targeted remediation, individual or collaborative practice activities and online investigations, peer conferencing and feedback, and recorded minilessons for each stage of a project. Although setting up stations involves thoughtful advance planning and group management strategies, stations free up precious teacher time for providing targeted feedback to advance the learning of all students. Many strategies for the essential teacher moves—asking probing questions, building schemas, and scaffolding strategically—can be the focus for a station. During extended projects, such as PBL, stations might include topics, such as how to generate questions for investigation, how to use sentence stems to support your writing, or how to set up a scrum board for your project.

Choice Boards, Assignment Menus, and Playlists. Similar to stations, these approaches require advance planning and offer a variety of activities related to the project or unit of study. The difference here is that *students* decide which activities they want to do. They might choose among three different ways to learn the same content (using podcasts, websites, or peer reading). If choice boards and playlists focus on a given format for the final product (a TED Talk, podcast, or blog), options might include watching a tutorial or using a step-by-step guide for those students who need more guidance. Students choose one product type from the menu, with the teacher providing support as needed. Be sure to offer options of increasing complexity.

In a given "menu," students select an appetizer, main course, side dish, and dessert. Let's look at an example using the novel *To Kill a Mockingbird*, which I have discussed elsewhere (Hess, 2018a, pp. 349–353):

- **Appetizers** introduce the topic or background information or ask students to summarize key points after listening, reading, or viewing material (DOK 2). For example, *Make a timeline of major events; Illustrate characters' emotions from a scene; Create three journal entries for a character reflecting on events.*

- **Main courses** offer ways for students to deepen conceptual understanding (DOK 3). For example, *In an essay, explain with text support why Atticus should or should not have taken the case; Write a letter to Harper Lee expressing your impressions of the book's themes, using text evidence to support your claims.*

- **Side dishes** offer tutorials (*how to conduct an interview*) and models for creating different products of learning (*how to design a website, create timelines, or draw maps*) (DOK 1–3).

- **Desserts** are rich learning opportunities requiring the deepest levels of thinking (DOK 3–4). For example, *Conduct a survey on peers' perspectives related to a theme (prejudice, human dignity, etc.); Analyze results, comparing the class's perspective with the novel's themes.*

You can use product choice boards over and over with different projects. Choice boards and assignment menus generally list up to nine different assignments (on a 3x3 grid) of varying complexity. Assignment menus usually include requirements as to how to make the choices—for example, there might be one required task and three optional assignments from each of three categories. This strategy appeals to student interests and strengths, giving students control over how they learn or demonstrate learning. (See more about the Choice Boards strategy in "Related Resources.")

Figure 5.9 shows a sample menu for remote learning. I created this for elementary schools I was working with during school shutdowns. Early in the week, teachers meet with their classes to review assignment options on the menu. The menu features links that students can click on for various materials they will need for the activities, and they share their work in weekly one-on-one conferences with the teacher.

FIGURE 5.9
Sample Menu for Remote Learning

Choice menu for the week of _____.
Choose one activity from each subject area.
Save your work for our weekly conferencing session.

Reading	Writing/ Social Studies	Science	Math	Fine Arts or Physical Education
Research this topic: _____. [Add links for suggested websites.] Write down five surprising facts you found, and explain why they surprised you.	Interview someone about what school was like when they were your age. Complete a Venn diagram to compare their experience with yours.	Fill water glasses with different levels of water. Gently tap each glass with a spoon. Record your observations about how the pitch changes with different amounts of water.	Use objects in your house to make three word problems. Each problem must use a different operation. Then show how to solve each one.	Record yourself showing the steps needed to make something, such as a craft project, or demonstrate your at-home exercise routine. [Add link for suggested ideas.]
Read an informational book or article. Write and illustrate a summary about what you learned.	Write a letter with an illustration to thank someone who helps others. [Add link for writing template.]	Take a walk with your family. Record signs of spring. Make predictions about how things will look in two weeks. [Add link for a recording sheet.]	Estimate how many cylinders you think you have in your house (soup cans, wastebaskets, etc.). Then count them to verify.	Do something nice for someone. Make a comic strip to tell and show what you did and how the person (or pet) reacted. [Add link for comic strip template.]

Stages 4 and 5. Interpret evidence and frame feedback; determine next steps to advance learning.

The One-Pager. I developed this idea to guide text-based discussions when teaching middle school decades ago. My students were reading novels, but not every student came to class having read the assigned homework. So one day I took a leap of faith, saying, "Today, you will be completing a one-pager." (My middle schoolers thought this should be easy—because it's only one page long.) At the top of the page, students select and copy a quote from the text. This starts everyone skimming the material. In the middle of the page, they explain why they chose the quote and how it connects to the central idea of the text. They may need to skim the text a second time to find a connection, or perhaps they decide to select a better quote. At the bottom, they create a visual to give meaning to the quote. In mathematics, a one-pager can show several ways to represent the same mathematical information, with students adding real-life examples or the steps they took to arrive at a solution. In history or science, a one-pager might illustrate cause and effect.

Fishbowl. Divide the class into two groups: An inside circle of students leads a discussion, and an outside group observes and provides feedback. Students in the inner circle prepare for discussion by reviewing resources and generating discussion questions. Sometimes the teacher provides an essential or a driving question to focus the discussion. Students in the outside circle can also "tap in," replacing someone on the inside after a few minutes. Teachers can use Fishbowl in any content domain to make problem solving and thinking visible.

Video Projects. A range of projects can use video to demonstrate both personal and academic learning. (See Appendix A, "Student-Friendly Tools," for a template to help students develop treatments, storyboards, and shooting scripts.) For a shorter classroom time frame or to introduce using video for storytelling, try assigning the Six-Word Memoir or Six-Word Story. Directions are simple: Students can use only six words or phrases to describe or introduce themselves, a person, or a character or to summarize a story line, event, or procedure. Students illustrate each word using a short video that features a series of still or moving pictures. They use storyboards to plan how to match the visuals with each of the six words. Students can practice the six-word strategy using TV commercials as inspiration for telling a concise story in less than 60 seconds.

Digital Storytelling. High school teacher Kimberly Hellerich (2021) introduces the concept of digital storytelling by asking students to analyze a poem by Walt Whitman. Next, students watch a three-minute YouTube video, "A Poetic Experiment: Walt Whitman, Interpreted by Three Animators" (www.youtube.com/watch?v=6jCw8ydqkrg) to illustrate different ways to interpret the poem using media. Seeing the same story through differing voices leads to increased empathy for others' points of view and deeper understanding of real-world issues. Students' final presentations incorporate photos or videos to tell a personal story. Digital storytelling is also an excellent vehicle for understanding historical topics and creating documentaries.

Stage 6. Use performance tasks to assess transfer and deepen learning.

Student-Developed Video Guides and Minilessons. Students can create videos to teach peers or demonstrate what they've learned. Tract: The Online Community Where Kids Teach Kids (https://teach.tract.app) offers numerous examples of student-created tutorials. The rule of thumb is to keep video tutorials under six minutes long with frequent shot changes (such as close-up, to long shot, to pan), a time frame that is based in research (Farah, 2020). Students can chunk a longer video lesson into two parts, inserting places to pause. For example, "Pause the video and try this now. Observe and record what happens. Then turn the video back on to see how to do the next step." Figure 5.10 offers a guide for developing short, student-produced minilessons or tutorials.

FIGURE 5.10

A Quick Guide for Developing Student-Created Minilessons

Identify your lesson focus and materials needed:

- What will you teach or explain?
- What tools, props, or visuals will you need?
- Do you need an assistant to demonstrate while you explain?
- Do you need to prepare a handout, diagram, or model?

Plan your script:

1. Introduce yourself and what you will teach or talk about.
2. Begin with a real-world connection, such as a question about something others may have observed or experienced (Have you ever noticed that _____? Have you ever wondered why or how _____? Would you like a better way to _____?).
3. Model, demonstrate, or do: Telling is not as effective as *showing* yourself (or another student) doing it while you're "thinking out loud" to describe what you're doing.
4. Add humor or gestures to engage the audience, but remember to stay focused on your topic.
5. End with a short summary of key points you just covered and something your audience might try or practice.
6. Rehearse, get feedback, keep timing under six minutes, and edit your script if needed.

Problem-Based Performance Tasks. Problem-based tasks are popular with teachers because they only take one to two class sessions to complete. Individual students or groups tackle a problem that requires evidence and reasoning to support the solution. Students can choose their problem-solving approach, the texts or tools they want to use, or how they will demonstrate learning. The STARS planning model is an excellent starting point for designing these tasks.

Begin by modeling the approach with students. Then, after scoring student work, select a few examples that represent highest to lowest scores. These samples can become anchor papers illustrating different levels of performance and different possible approaches. Students can use anchor papers to annotate each part of an exemplary student response or compare two sample responses to identify strong as opposed to weak supporting evidence.

Here are some examples of problem-based task prompts in a variety of subject areas:

- **Science.** What kind of objects float? What kind sink? Choose 10 objects to test in the water tank. List each object on your recording sheet. Then check "sink" or "float" next to each to show your predictions. Test each object and record the results. Did the object sink or float? Use your data to describe what happened. What did you learn about objects that float and objects that sink? Do you see any patterns? Did anything surprise you?

- **Math.** Study the map of this island. A treasure chest is buried somewhere. Unfortunately, the pirates didn't include enough information about the treasure's location, making it difficult to find. Use the information provided to determine measurements between objects on the map. Then write specific directions from where your boat is docked to the exact location of the treasure. Explain how you determined the measurements and why you think your directions are correct.

- **Graphic design.** Make changes to an existing design and provide evidence to show how these changes will improve the overall quality or message of the final product or appeal to a different audience.

- **Language arts.** You have been asked to make a recommendation to the school board about whether or not to change the starting time of school. Use the playlist provided to select at least two articles about school starting times for teens. Read or listen to the media messages, take notes, and decide what position you support. Prepare a letter or presentation that clearly articulates your claim, provides supporting reasoning and evidence, and dispels any counterclaims.

- **Science.** (This prompt is adapted from a Stanford Center of Assessment, Learning, and Equity [SCALE] performance task, "Deer Population.") Scientists have noticed a big change in the number of deer in Colorado and have collected several types of data related to this change. Study the data provided, look for patterns, and identify possible causes. Then write a claim describing the most likely cause of the change, providing supporting reasoning, relevant data from the figures, and your knowledge of what organisms need to survive within an ecosystem (See SCALE, "Related Resources.")

- **Economics.** Various types of economies make up our daily lives. Use what you learned in yesterday's activities to explain how aspects of traditional, command, and market economies have become part of your life. Then identify which type of economy has had the most influence on your life and explain your reasoning, using specific evidence.

Inquiry-Based Investigations. Watching teacher-selected video excerpts (for example, from TV shows like *MythBusters* and *How'd They Do That?*) is one way to illustrate how real-world inquiry-based investigations can begin with a curious question. Active learning is driven by student-generated questions and research, leading to critical thinking, creative design, and problem solving.

At the elementary level, a teacher will often begin with a strategy such as KWHL to guide a whole-class investigation, modeling how to generate and narrow down the investigation questions, locate resources, and decide how to conduct research. Initially, stations might guide each stage of the investigations; ultimately, small groups will take more control of their investigations using a familiar step-by-step protocol supported by teacher coaching. At the secondary level, students might analyze a case study, with teachers providing guiding questions for discussion and research. As students become more familiar with inquiry-based investigations throughout the year, they can advance from *structured inquiry* to *coached inquiry* to *free inquiry*, generating their own questions for investigations and determining how to share their learning publicly. Figure 5.11 shows the various steps for inquiry-based investigations.

Project-Based Learning. Project-based learning integrates core academics into investigations of real-world problems or issues using extended projects. Unlike Problem-Based Performance Tasks and Inquiry-Based Investigations that are often embedded into a unit of study, PBL *is* the unit of study; here, the teacher is assessing both the processes used during the project and the products of learning. Because a PBL can take several weeks of instructional time, it's crucial to ensure that it addresses and assesses core academic standards. Teachers implementing PBL usually start by replacing an existing standards-based

FIGURE 5.11
Steps for Developing Inquiry-Based Investigations

1. **Explore a broad topic of interest or analyze a case study.**
   a. Identify what is already known about the topic.
   b. Generate questions to investigate or hypotheses to test.
   c. Decide if you will work alone or in a group.

2. **Delve deeper into the topic to narrow the focus.**
   a. Explore resources, take notes, and discuss with others.
   b. Narrow the focus, and revise research questions or hypotheses.
   c. Set a goal for sharing your learning (e.g., to teach others, create an informational pamphlet, build and test a prototype, or create a documentary).

3. **Conduct research.**
   a. Plan the investigation. (Suggested planning tools: Student-Designed Investigations with Checkpoints, Writing Treatments and Developing Shooting Scripts, or Project Planning by DOK Levels in Appendix A; or the Collaborative Inquiry Planning Tool in Chapter 3)
   b. Locate sources, check the accuracy and credibility of sources, and take notes.
   c. Gather and organize your notes and materials, and create supporting visuals for the final product.
   d. Create and test ideas; collect data, get feedback, and revise ideas.

4. **Refine the final product and present what you learned.**

unit of study with what they believe is a more engaging approach to learning the same academic skills and concepts.

Because PBLs are somewhat complex to design from scratch, it makes sense to explore the many high-quality resources available to find a sample that fits your curriculum (see "Related Resources" for some suggestions). Regardless of the model you choose, all PBLs have similar design features: They're intellectually challenging; they offer an authentic, real-world context; they require project management skills; they involve collaboration and student voice and choice; they presuppose a public sharing of the products beyond the classroom; and they require students to reflect on what and how they have learned. You might use backward design to create a PBL that assesses specific skills or, alternatively, select a real-world problem of interest to students before deciding which skills and concepts are most appropriate to address.

To launch the PBL and give it a real-world context, provide relevant entry events, such as media clips, documentaries, photos, stories, expert speakers, field trips, or explorations of local areas. Collaboration activities require many interpersonal and intrapersonal skills that both teachers and students can assess. Teams of students might have a project manager in charge of setting up and monitoring the scrum board or maintaining a project log. Public sharing of learning can range from informal (such as posting on a blog) to more formal formats (such as doing a presentation for a panel to evaluate).

What's the Story or What's My Story? This inquiry-based project frames a longer study of an issue of compelling interest to students. It begins with students choosing a topic (such as pollution, equity, or social justice); identifying a related problem or driving question with support from the teacher ("Does everyone in our community have access to healthcare?"); conducting an investigation; and, finally, telling "the story" using a short video. This extended project idea comes from the Vermont Young People Social Action Team's "What's the Story?" project (see "Related Resources").

Genius Hour. Because Genius Hour assessments are not as structured as Problem-Based Performance Tasks or Project-Based Learning, teachers need to use several management strategies to keep students focused and on track. For example, project planning documents, video guides, or choice boards can guide stages of the work. Teachers can offer minilessons to support project management strategies or how-to sessions for developing different products, including sharing examples of past student-developed products. Conferencing with individuals or small groups also enables teachers to provide resources, track progress, or provide scaffolding. Although Genius Hour is driven by student questions, task-neutral scoring rubrics can focus on procedures such as researching, planning, and sharing products of learning, as well as on self-direction skills. (See "Related Resources" for more guidance.)

Global Challenge. In the early 1990s, Grant Wiggins invited me to be part of an outside review panel for elementary students presenting what they had learned about a topic of interest. That practice is still going strong in many New Jersey schools. For example, Wise and McTighe (2017) describe a weeklong, interdisciplinary project in New Jersey's West Windsor–Plainsboro Regional School District in which students choose a global challenge they are passionate about and develop questions to explore by listening to podcasts and interviewing experts in the field. Teachers provide resources, guide planning when needed, and document their observations while students are working. Final presentations are judged by members from business and the community who receive training in success criteria before giving feedback to students. Rubrics stress the importance of assessing the "impact" of the students' message about the global challenge through creating awareness campaigns or suggesting solutions to existing problems.

To Sum Up

Figure 5.12 summarizes how you might apply the strategies described in this chapter to deepen understanding using increasingly complex performance tasks. Many of the

FIGURE 5.12

Actionable Strategies for Complex Tasks That Transfer Learning

Actionable Assessment Cycle Stages	Strategies	Primary Purpose	Look Fors: Students who engage with complex performance-based assessments (PBAs) . . .
1. Clarify learning targets.	Essential Questions	Frame a unit of study or plan a lesson focus.	Use essential or driving questions to focus learning, guide inquiry, and develop relevant products and self-reflections.
	Driving Questions	Launch project-based learning/PBL.	
2. Embed short-cycle formative tasks into instruction.	"Reading" Visuals	Introduce content, build background knowledge, generate questions.	Use visual information to draw inferences and raise questions for investigation.
	Ask Three Sources	Locate potential resources for a project, build background knowledge.	Use multiple types of sources to conduct research.
	Graffiti Boards	Respond to a question, data, artifacts, photos, current events, etc.	Generate possible questions or solutions, or identify differing perspectives.
3. Uncover thinking and document evidence of learning.	Anticipation Guides	Practice formulating opinions, documenting supporting evidence.	Use evidence and reasoning to support claims.
	Station Differentiation Station Rotations	Offer choice activities for different groups, or have groups cycle through the same activities.	Complete multistep tasks.
	Assignment Menus Playlists Choice Boards	Offer choices of different complexity levels and interest; may include assignment and product choices.	Choose and complete tasks of increasing complexity.
4. Interpret evidence and frame feedback. *and* 5. Determine next steps to advance learning.	One-Pagers	Respond visually to interpret quotes, texts, processes, etc.	Visually represent interpretations of complex ideas.
	Fishbowl	Students prepare for and lead discussions; peers critique and give feedback.	Prepare for and collaboratively discuss complex issues using reasoning and supporting evidence.
	Six-Word Memoir Six-Word Story Digital Storytelling	Shorter video projects demonstrating what students have learned.	Visually represent interpretations of complex ideas.

(continued)

FIGURE 5.12
Actionable Strategies for Complex Tasks That Transfer Learning (*continued*)

Actionable Assessment Cycle Stages	Strategies	Primary Purpose	Look Fors: Students who engage with complex performance-based assessments (PBAs) . . .
6. Use performance tasks to assess transfer and deepen learning.	Video Guides and Minilessons What's My Story? What's the Story?	Video projects demonstrating what students have learned.	Complete multistep tasks or projects. Use multimedia to share products of learning. Investigate open-ended questions of personal interest.
	Problem-Based Tasks Inquiry-Based Investigations Project-Based Learning/PBL Global Challenge	Encourages disciplined inquiry with collaborative planning, researching, and public sharing of products.	
	Wonder of the Day (less complex; see Chapter 4) Genius Hour	Encourages disciplined inquiry on topics of interest. Students generate questions and topics. Students work alone or with others.	Generate and investigate questions of personal interest.

strategies discussed in earlier chapters will prepare students for completing complex, multi-day performance assessments.

In Chapter 6, we'll consider the last of the five essential teacher moves—engage students in metacognition throughout the learning process.

RELATED RESOURCES

- **BEST Toolkits**
  www.best-future.org/resources

- **BEST K–12 Collaboration Rubrics**
  www.karin-hess.com/archived-postings

- **Choice Boards for English Language Arts**
  https://goopennc.oercommons.org/courseware/lesson/5878/overview

- **Choice Board Templates for Google Slides or PowerPoint**
  https://slidesmania.com/tag/choice-boards

- **Defined Learning: High-Quality Project-Based Learning for All**
  www.definedlearning.com

- **Exemplars**
  www.exemplars.com

- **Facing History and Ourselves Teaching (strategies, resources, and videos)**
  www.facinghistory.org

- **Free Technology for Teachers by Richard Byrne**
  www.freetech4teachers.com

- **Genius Hour, Design Thinking, and More by A. J. Juliani**
  www.ajjuliani.com/blog

- **Hess Assessment Development Tools**
  www.karin-hess.com/formative-and-performance-assessments

- **Integrating Social-Emotional Learning with Project-Based Learning by Mike Kaechele**
  www.michaelkaechele.com

- **KQED Learn Youth Media Challenges**
  www.kqed.org/education/collection/youth-media-challenges

- **PBL Works**
  www.pblworks.org

- **PBL Works for Remote Learning**
  www.pblworks.org/pbl-remote-learning

- **Project-Based Learning, Genius Hour, and Distance Learning by John Spencer**
  www.spencerauthor.com

- **Project-Based Learning Planning Guide (for elementary grades)**
  www.performingeducation.com/planningguide

- **Project-Based Learning and Powerful Instructional Practices**
  www.sreb.org/powerful-instructional-practices

- **Project-Based Learning Projects and Teaching Strategies by Todd Stanley**
  www.thegiftedguy.com/resources

- **"Projects and PBL: What's the Difference?" (video)**
  www.youtube.com/watch?v=dhwuQU2-g5g

- **"The Power of Performance Assessments: Oakland Unified's Graduate Capstone Project" (video)**
  www.youtube.com/watch?v=V5ts4gZSux8

- **Stanford NGSS Assessment Design and Analysis Resources**
  https://scienceeducation.stanford.edu/snap/ngss-assessment-design-and-analysis-resources

- **Stanford Instructionally Embedded Assessments**
  https://scienceeducation.stanford.edu/assessment/instructionally-embedded-assessments

- **"Starting Your Podcast: A Guide for Students"**
  www.npr.org/2018/11/15/662070097/starting-your-podcast-a-guide-for-students

- **"Tools to Help Students Base Opinions in Fact" by Curtis Chandler**
  www.middleweb.com/44136/tools-to-help-students-base-opinions-in-fact

- **Tract: The Online Community Where Kids Teach Kids**
  https://teach.tract.app

- **We Teach NYC**
  www.weteachnyc.org

- **What's the Story? The Vermont Young People Social Action Team**
  www.whatsthestory.middcreate.net/vermont

6

Engage Students in Metacognition and Reflection

Metacognition breeds agency. Students who are practicing reflection, goal-setting, and then monitoring and adapting their actions based on this ongoing process begin to take ownership in a way that exemplifies an empowered learner.

—Jonathan G. Vander Els and Brian M. Stack, *Unpacking the Competency-Based Classroom*

The fifth essential teacher move to deepen learning is to engage students in metacognition and reflection activities—not as an afterthought, but as crucial to students becoming independent learners. The phrases *metacognitive skills* and *self-reflection* are often used interchangeably, and although they're interrelated, they're not the same. Metacognition happens "in the moment" during learning; reflection is the act of looking back on past learning, determining the meaning of what was learned; building (or not building) confidence as a learner; and carrying that mindset forward. Metacognitive skills are helpful for staying focused and monitoring progress during learning. Peer and self-reflection activities help learners identify their strengths and challenges and set and evaluate achievement of personal goals for learning. Educators sometimes assess the use of metacognition through direct observation, checklists, and conferencing. However, the most powerful assessment is when students can attend closely to their own learning, knowing what evidence to look for that tells them they're making progress and deciding how best to move forward. In other words, metacognitive students understand that they're on a learning path and that they're in some control of where that path leads.

Rigor by design is only relevant and meaningful when it is student-centered. Teacher moves are teacher-driven in that each teacher can create opportunities for students to ask their own driving questions, build their own mental schemas, and acquire scaffolding skills they can use independently when tackling complex tasks in the future. Developing metacognitive and self-reflection skills is the icing on the cake; doing so is integral to becoming a self-directed learner who can propel and personalize learning in and out of school.

The Role of Engagement

As you may recall from Chapter 1, emotional engagement (being open, interested, and curious) generally comes before and supports deeper cognitive engagement (the ability to self-monitor, make connections, or seek relevance). As Frey and Fisher (2021) note, "One who is cognitively but not affectively engaged may lack the will to persist when learning gets more difficult. And a learner who is only emotionally engaged may feel great interest in the subject but put forth little effort" (p. 2).

Rigor by design brings engagement into greater focus. You have probably observed students who did what you asked of them, as well as those who went out of their way to avoid or actively disrupt the flow of learning in the classroom. When any of these behaviors are present, there is little hope that students will be invested in or introspective about their learning. Students who are simply compliant are not necessarily interested in taking control of their learning. "Just tell me what to do" and "Is this what you want?" are indicators that students are only minimally engaged, if at all. A small number of students may thrive on learning and go above and beyond the teacher's expectations most of the time, but those students are not the norm. As a matter of fact, many teachers do not believe that most of their students *can* become fully engaged most of the time. To some degree, this is probably true if students have only learned how to do what the teacher has asked them to do—or coerced them into doing so.

Frey and Fisher (2021) created a visual to explain Amy Berry's 2020 research interpreting teachers' perceptions of student engagement in the classroom. The continuum in Figure 6.1 shows that students can be actively disengaged or actively engaged during learning. In between these two extremes are the students who are passively engaged. Passive learners are rewarded for completing their assignments. They often fly under the radar, fooling educators into thinking that if they're not acting out, they're probably learning something.

FIGURE 6.1
A Continuum of Engagement

Active ←			Passive ——→		Active
Disrupt	**Avoid**	**Withdraw**	**Participate**	**Invest**	**Drive**
Distract others Disrupt learning activities	Avoid working Stay off task unless prompted	Become easily distracted Physically separate from group	Complete assignments Pay attention Answer questions	Ask questions Seek value and relevance in learning	Set and monitor goals Seek and use feedback Self-assess
Disengagement			**Engagement**		
Students who are "checked out"			Students who are "checked in"		

Source: Adapted from "New Thinking About Student Engagement," by D. Fisher and N. Frey, 2021, *Educational Leadership, 79*(4). https://www.ascd.org/el/articles/show-and-tell-a-video-column-new-thinking-about-student-engagement

Berry's research concluded that as students became more engaged, they learned more. This seemed to be true even when students only increased their engagement incrementally, such as by moving from "avoiding" to "withdrawing" or from "withdrawing" to "participating."

Teachers can increase the active engagement of every student in two ways. First, help them understand and recognize the behaviors depicted in the continuum so that they can self-monitor their own engagement. Second, provide ongoing opportunities for metacognitive and reflective activities that teach students how to be actively engaged—to set and monitor goals, use peer conferencing to improve the quality of their work, and collect evidence that demonstrates personal progress. Students who can *see* their own progress are more motivated to improve their performance than they are when they simply hear encouragement from supportive adults (Hess, 2018a).

Learning to Self-Assess Engagement

When remote learning was the only option for school being in session, teachers in some schools in which I worked discovered that engagement was key to unlocking learning. They also found that it took a village—working transparently with students—to increase active engagement in both their remote and in-person classrooms. Teachers cocreated a version of Berry's research-based continuum with their students, asking them to discuss, describe, and draw what each level of engagement looked like using examples from their own classroom. Students also considered the reasons why they might be more or less engaged. Now, students had a kid-friendly way to assess their engagement. At first, they used their "customized" rubrics (based on Figure 6.1) as a quick self- or class assessment at the end of a lesson and followed up by setting a short-term engagement goal to revisit in the next lesson. Eventually, the class used group and self-assessments periodically within the context of more complex work (answering questions such as, *How did your level of engagement affect your work? How engaged were members of your team?*). Teachers set the compass for deeper learning by holding students accountable for being engaged and by providing outlets (for example, conferencing with peers or the teacher) for them to express what was and wasn't working. (See "Related Resources" for "Show & Tell," an ASCD video of a high school teacher using a Jigsaw to introduce Berry's engagement continuum to his students.)

Discourse and Collaboration Strategies That Help

Sometimes teachers tell me that they don't use self-reflection and peer critiques because their students don't know how to self-assess beyond using a checklist or how to be respectful when giving peers feedback. These inter- and intrapersonal skills will not develop by chance; you must teach them, and students must practice them regularly. My advice is simple:

- Get students to understand what active engagement looks and sounds like, and then have them self-assess their engagement.
- Get students to actively engage with peers in productive group work.
- Ask students to use a variety of metacognitive skills and reflection activities to evaluate their individual roles within a group and the effectiveness of group processes.

Using the GPS–I Rule to Structure Productive Group Work

Many people can remember some not-so-great experiences working in groups. Sometimes, one person dominated the conversation or was not respectful when interacting with others, or one person got stuck doing all the work while everyone got credit for it. If you were willing to be the workhorse of the group, everyone wanted to be in your group.

The seminal work of Johnson and Johnson (1975) on group creativity is of great value here. I've adapted their principles to create the GPS–I Rule when structuring group work, which is equally effective for both students and adults. The initialism is a useful way to remember the research related to designing successful and productive group collaborations:

- **Group processing.** Group members begin by establishing norms to guide their work—norms they all agree to follow (such as encouraging everyone to contribute, taking turns, refraining from making negative comments, designating roles to complete the work, and turning off cell phones). Each time the group meets, they quickly review norms before getting started. Groups then clarify their tasks, set goals, and assign roles to accomplish the tasks. On completion, the members *collaboratively reflect on how well they worked together*. How did they solve problems when members didn't agree? Did they listen to suggestions that improved the quality of their work? Did everyone contribute? Group members can use quick hand signals or emojis to show how well they think their group worked together that day. Finally, group members set a goal for how they'll work together (or improve) next time. They might also revise the group norms. Group processing ensures that the group—not the teacher—holds members accountable.

- **Positive interdependence.** Group norms should address *positive interdependence*— that is, group members depending on one another to accomplish a shared goal. Positive interdependence includes how members interact with and encourage one another and how each person's task depends on another person completing their part. For example, if two students are developing a storyboard, one person might verify types of camera shots to use and the other might draft the shooting script for the documentary they're producing. Teachers can foster interdependence by having each student use a different resource or search for different pieces of information needed to solve the problem or complete the task. One student might research the context of a historical event, while others look for differing perspectives, causes, or effects of the event. Then they combine and analyze the information together to develop a role-play depicting the event.

- **Simultaneous engagement.** When forming groups, consider the number of roles needed to complete the given tasks. A student in a group with too many members may become disengaged because there are more members than roles to fulfill. Roles should demonstrate that everyone is working on something and contributing to the group's shared goal. Rather than pre-assigning roles, teachers might describe the roles needed and let students decide who will be responsible for each role or ask groups to break tasks down to determine how each member can contribute. Roles establish how each individual will be held accountable within the group. *Simultaneous* *engagement* means that everyone is working and contributing at the same time, not that some members are waiting around to do a task that comes at the end, like reporting the group's progress. Simultaneous engagement and positive interdependence help students learn the social skills that enable them to be emotionally and cognitively engaged, face-to-face or remotely.

- **Individual accountability.** Both the group and each individual are accountable for their contributions. Thinking through the task requirements together helps students clarify and take responsibility for answering this question: *What is my group supposed to do, and how will I contribute so that we can accomplish it together successfully?* This raises the age-old issue of grading group work. Teachers can assess individual contributions separately from the group's final product *if* they have designed rubrics for both aspects of group work. Teachers sometimes rotate roles, such as in a course in videography, so that by the end of the year, every student has demonstrated knowledge and skills in each role. No one is held accountable for every role on every project, however. When students rotate roles, they can also teach peers what they have already learned about how to do that job effectively.

Figure 6.2 shows an excerpt from the BEST Collaboration Rubrics, K–12 (see "Related Resources"), describing the highest performance level ("extending") for each grade span. Self-reflection and peer assessments require students to provide their own supporting evidence to demonstrate that they have met expectations. The criterion for *self-awareness* addresses personal responsibility within a group; the criterion for monitoring and adapting addresses group processing and positive interdependence within the group. Using rubric descriptors like the one shown in Figure 6.2 can guide students in identifying supporting evidence.

You can structure collaboration, engagement, and meaningful discourse by ensuring the following:

- **Start with an authentic task worth doing.** Working in groups shouldn't mean working on low-level tasks (near transfer). Students can do most familiar routine tasks (DOK 1 and 2) quite efficiently on their own. When you want students to do something challenging—perhaps more challenging than individual students are able to accomplish on their own—having them work in groups is an excellent opportunity for them to take risks, struggle through a problem, and learn together as they construct deeper levels of meaning. After all, "under the right circumstances, groups are remarkably intelligent and are often smarter than the smartest people in them" (Surowiecki, 2005, p. xiii).

FIGURE 6.2

Indicators of Collaboration at the "Extending" Performance Level

Grade Spans	Self-Assessment Self-Awareness and Personal Responsibility I can . . .	Peer Assessment Monitoring and Adapting I can . . .
K–2	Reflect on what I did well, what I'm getting better at, and what I learned from working with my group.	Work with my group to suggest ways to improve how we work together as a group (e.g., using a peer conferencing rubric).
3–5	Reflect on what I learned working with my group when I used my strengths and challenged myself.	Reflect with my group on progress we made and what we learned from working out problems or challenges together.
6–8	Describe how I contributed my strengths and overcame challenges to improve the quality of my group's final product.	Work with my group to reflect on group progress and adapt norms, roles, or strategies to optimize the collective group effort and advance the overall quality of my group's performance.
9–12	Analyze how my roles and responsibilities within the group dynamics demonstrated individual responsibility and enhanced group equity.	Work with my group to reflect on group progress and adapt norms, roles, or strategies to optimize the collective group effort and enhance a positive group dynamic.

Source: From "Collaboration Rubrics (Grades K–2; Grades 3–5; Grades 6–8; Grades 9–12)," *Toolkits & Resources*, by BEST for the Future, 2022. https://best-future.org/resources/. Adapted with permission.

- **Be sure everyone has a job.** We can maximize simultaneous engagement and support deeper understanding when we structure group work for complex tasks that require a stretch (far transfer). To do this well, we need to answer two questions: (1) What is the purpose (intended learning) of the project or performance-based task? and (2) How many people will it take to successfully complete it? Educators can encourage group members to self-assign roles for each job by guiding them in breaking down and defining possible tasks that will lead to successful completion. Groups can assign roles based on individual skills, talents, or personal interests, or by lottery, when all else fails. (See Collaborative Inquiry Planning, Chapter 3.)
- **Establish parameters for completing the task.** We often give too great of a time frame and too little direction as to what we expect students to do. Saying, "Discuss this with the person next to you" is not as clear as saying, "You have one minute to discuss and write three reasons why _____." Whether it's a short, informal group

sharing (Turn-and-Talk, Think-Pair-Share) or a longer performance or project-based task taking several days, giving students an estimated time frame and clear success criteria holds everyone accountable for managing the work, staying on task, and getting it done. Remember, you can always give groups more time if they need it.

Many of the group discourse and peer conferencing strategies described in earlier chapters support increased engagement and productive group work. Peer-assisted learning, such as composing a text together, and peer conferencing strategies (such as the 20-Minute Peer Feedback System, Carousel Feedback, and Scrum Boards) teach students how to respectfully give and receive feedback, which are important life skills.

Self-Reflection—By Design

The word *assess* derives from the Latin *assidere*, meaning to sit beside a learner. So when teachers say that their students don't do a good job of self-assessment, I immediately wonder *how* they're asking students to self-assess or reflect on their learning. Are students using checklists because checklists take less time to complete than having the teacher "sit beside" students to conference? Are students using rubrics with vague or subjective terms or mostly negative descriptors at the lower performance levels? I don't know anyone who wants to use negative language to self-assess their learning, especially if they're novices learning something new. Have teachers modeled what self-reflection looks like, including how they made decisions along the way or how they turned a mistake into new learning? Constructing meaning about how learning has personally affected a learner doesn't happen by chance; it happens by design. There are no shortcuts to self-reflection, but there are some clear pathways.

Self-direction is a complex competency that includes both the intrapersonal skills of self-awareness and reflection and the interpersonal skill of collaboration. When exercising self-direction skills, students identify their interests about the topic under study, collaborate with and seek input from others, and apply ideas to shape their learning process. This includes setting goals for learning, crafting driving questions for inquiry, drawing on previous learning to guide decisions, reassessing and adjusting an approach after getting feedback, managing the work to meet agreed-on deadlines, and attending to the quality of their work. Seeking assistance is not a weakness; it's a sign of student agency and being self-aware of oneself as a learner.

Research (Lench et al., 2015) identifies five interrelated components of self-direction:

- **Self-awareness.** Reflecting on past experiences to evaluate one's strengths, limitations, motivation, interests, and aspirations within different learning contexts: *What am I learning about myself as a learner?*

- **Initiative and ownership.** Taking responsibility for learning, finding purposeful driving questions, shaping opportunities to fit personal interests and learning style, and seeking input from others: *How can I integrate my personal interests into how I approach new learning?*

- **Goal setting and planning.** Developing long-term goals, establishing meaningful learning targets, identifying effective strategies, and planning out steps: *Am I able to break down a complex task and develop concrete steps to accomplish it?*

- **Engaging and managing.** Seeking relevant resources and information to support learning goals and refining strategies; maintaining an effective pace and reaching short-term benchmarks and long-term goals: *What am I learning about locating resources, managing my time, and seeking help when I need it?*

- **Monitoring and adapting.** Evaluating progress, adapting strategies, seizing failure to grow from mistakes, and attributing success to effort and motivation: *Am I able to see when something isn't working well, adjust my approach, and learn from missteps?*

Although each component could be viewed as a stand-alone skill, each provides a unique contribution to developing self-direction. Learners often demonstrate more advanced behaviors with some components than with others, so assessing the components using a rubric with numerical scores is not as meaningful as having students identify where they are along a continuum—including why they think they're there, and how they might move forward. Positive, nonjudgmental language in student-friendly rubrics clarifies expectations for both learners and educators.

When educators know what to look for and when students understand how to "look back" and reflect on their learning, a beautiful thing happens. Students provide insights into their learning and thinking processes that we can only guess at. Structuring self-reflection activities can range from providing sentence starters for sharing learning or getting feedback, to giving students open-ended prompts related to self-direction components, to student-led conferences and portfolio defenses.

Reflecting on the Final Product

Imagine that students have been reading and discussing dystopian literature as part of a middle school unit of study. The readings prepare students to develop their final product—an infographic depicting a modern-day dystopia (a speculated community or society that is undesirable or frightening). The students have learned that to create a "good" dystopia, it must be believable and it has to be scary—it's a dystopia, not a utopia!—and there must be options for improving it.

Students select the real-world problem they want to address, investigate and narrow their focus, and decide how to visually present the topic. For example, one student who was concerned about the loss of the rain forest created an infographic about a world weakened by environmental damage. In my workshops, I show an example of a student's final product and ask participants to identify the skills and concepts they think the student has transferred to create the infographic. Then I share the student's self-reflection essay and ask, "What new information did you just discover that you could not have learned from only assessing the final product?" This exercise reinforces the importance of assessing not only the products of learning, but also the *processes* of learning.

Now I will ask you the same question. Even without seeing a final product, what can you learn from sample reflective journal entries in Figure 6.3 about the student's thinking processes that show evidence of far transfer in developing the dystopia infographic? Each entry responds to a given prompt.

In a classroom, students can annotate examples of student self-reflections from previous years to understand how to create their own self-reflection, which they can share as a written essay, a visual or multimedia display, an oral presentation (live or recorded), or part of a student-led conference or portfolio defense. Whenever possible, give students the opportunity to choose a personally meaningful way to reflect on their learning.

Applying Metacognition and Reflection to the Actionable Assessment Cycle

Several strategies we have already discussed can serve a dual purpose with metacognition or reflection. When students Sketchnote (Chapter 3), for example, they are actively thinking metacognitively about how they connect ideas. When they create a Six-Word Memoir (Chapter 5) to introduce themselves, they are reflecting on and expressing how they see themselves as learners. Conferencing, collaborating, and reflecting and self-assessing using a rubric all work toward this end.

FIGURE 6.3
Sample Reflective Journal Entries

Prompt 1. How did you determine your focus?

To create my infographic, I first researched my topic. I had a relatively easy topic to find information on, and it was not too hard to find hard statistics to use. I had to figure out in what direction I was going with the information, be it focusing on the United States, or animals, or the world. I picked the rain forest for how tremendous the loss is and some general facts overall.

Prompt 2. How will your infographic reflect what you learned and have an effect on readers?

Once I had my facts, I had to figure out how to present them in a visually pleasing way. The layout I chose is good for environmental damage because first I explained the topic, then showed the damage, and then showed how to fix it. Environmental damage is such a serious and fast-moving issue, especially in the United States. The damage affects the future. In dystopian literature, environmental damage is almost always a main source for the beginning of the "end" or the collapse of the media [people no longer have access to the truth].

Prompt 3. What insights are you starting to develop?

Looking at the data of our real-life damage is frightening. The proven data about today's world and the environmental damage could suggest a reason for the world to become a dystopian society, just like in all the books. This is such a scary thought, and barely anyone seems to really care. That is also a big theme of the United States and the world: living for today and not tomorrow.

Prompt 4. How are you drawing on/transferring your prior knowledge? What decisions did you make to create your final product?

The first thing I added to my infographic is an eye-appealing graphic of the world behind the title. The reason it is green is because the central color that connects with environment is green. The background is black to symbolize trauma, death, and havoc. From the world graphic and title "Environmental Damage" you can really infer what this infographic will be about, and it gives a good first impression.

The next thing I added was a blurb about what climate change is and how it affects [the world] today. I wanted to start with a little introduction so that people will have the important prior knowledge they need, very similar to an introduction paragraph in an essay. I made all the text with information white because it contrasts well with black.

The next thing I chose to add was the damage that has already been done to the world. I did this because I wanted to evoke emotional reactions from the viewers and show the hard facts of the damage. After I show the damage, I show how to help [alleviate] the damage. This is a good order because since viewers are already feeling bad for what has happened, this gives them motivation to do some of the suggested things to help.

Let's now look at metacognition and reflection in terms of the six stages of the Actionable Assessment Cycle.

Stage 1. Clarify learning targets.

Asking learners to make connections between what they've learned and larger ideas related to the essential or driving question provides insights into, and clear evidence of, learning transfer. Prompts for self-reflection include asking students to demonstrate how the learning relates to broader ideas beyond the unit of study or product they created.

Teachers can use descriptors from existing rubrics to develop self-reflection prompts and scoring criteria for student-led conferences and portfolio defenses.

Figure 6.4 illustrates how teachers turned two criteria from the "expanding" performance level into prompts that students in grades 9–12 can use to locate work samples as evidence of learning when preparing for presentations or conferencing. (See "Related Resources" for BEST Toolkits, which include Creative Thinking Rubrics.)

FIGURE 6.4
Self-Reflection Prompts for Creative Thinking and Creative Products

Self-Awareness
Prompt: Analyze and provide examples of how using creative problem-solving processes helped you pursue personal interests, seek out supportive resources or environments, or share ideas or products that positively affect others.
Tolerating Risk Ambiguity
Prompt: Evaluate the effects of the approaches you used and the decisions you made throughout the creative process. Then explain how you might apply your new learning or insights to challenge established social, cultural, or artistic norms.

Source: From "Collaboration Rubrics (Grades K–2; Grades 3–5; Grades 6–8; Grades 9–12)," *Toolkits & Resources,* by BEST for the Future, 2022. https://best-future.org/resources/. Adapted with permission.

Stage 2. Embed short-cycle formative tasks into instruction.

Roll the Dice. When students critique or give feedback on the work of their peers, they naturally have to reflect on what they know, using an understanding of the related success criteria. This quick strategy uses a cube with a different question on each side for students to practice giving feedback to peers. Either the teacher or small groups roll the die to see what the focus of the feedback will be. For example, after students solve a performance task in mathematics, a roll of the dice might reveal questions like these (based on rubric criteria): *Are calculations, labels, and terms accurate (DOK 1)? Is the graph, table, or diagram accurate, complete, and useful in showing the math relationships in the problem (DOK 2)? Does the reasoning explain how the calculations, representations, and strategy used all support the solution (DOK 3)? Is a related mathematical connection made between the problem and a math concept or real-world application (DOK 2)? Is there an error? Explain how you know, or how you would correct it and why (DOK 3).* In social studies, each side of the cube might address a question about products or sources used during research.

Feedback Stems. If the objective of giving feedback is to help someone improve their performance—remember, you're "sitting beside" the learner—then it's important to teach and model for students the difference between telling someone what is wrong with their work and providing descriptive feedback in relation to success criteria. Feedback is "actionable" when it targets something specific, guiding the learner to decide whether to keep the work as is or do something that will improve it. Feedback stems guide students in using descriptive language, along with specific examples related to success criteria, when giving such feedback. Actionable feedback identifies where a student is on the learning continuum (or rubric) and helps the receiver of the feedback figure out ways to move forward.

Figure 6.5 provides examples of descriptive and actionable feedback stems. Students can generate their own examples to add to a few that the teacher has modeled to create their own lists. Teachers might post the feedback stems in the classroom as a reminder when conferencing, or students can have personal "feedback cheat sheets" on hand at their desks. Feedback stems are also useful to adults when reviewing and giving feedback to peers about draft performance assessments or unit planning.

Metacognitive Bookmarks. Teachers of reading have used this effective "as-you-read" strategy for many years. As with chunking a text, stopping to make notes on a physical bookmark while reading helps students maintain focus, consolidate learning, and build stamina for engaging with longer texts. Each bookmark has a focus, such as identifying strategies to make sense of the text or identifying examples of how an author uses figurative language. Beers and Probst (2013) have applied this approach to reading both literary and nonfiction texts as a way for students to practice a given strategy. For example, students who are learning about how statistics are used in scientific texts might read a text to locate and explain (on the bookmark) how the statistics in the text support the ideas presented. You can also use bookmark prompts to prepare students for a group discussion; guide entries in a learning log; or support students when they annotate texts, interpreting multiple text signals or signposts that aid comprehension. The greatest advantage of using the Metacognitive Bookmarks strategy is when students read the same text several times for different purposes to build a deeper understanding. Completing a graphic organizer with information involving multiple signposts or using a jigsaw strategy with groups focusing on different aspects of a text are other ways to adapt this metacognitive strategy.

Stage 3. Uncover thinking and document evidence of learning.

Interactive Checkpoints. Interactive checkpoints create an informal dialogue between the learner and those giving feedback. One use of the strategy is with longer multistep performance tasks, such as breaking down a student-designed science investigation into smaller parts, with checkpoints along the way. After completing each part, students receive feedback to determine whether they are ready to move on or need to make corrections before beginning the next part. (See Appendix A for an example of a science investigation with built-in interactive checkpoints.) Teachers can complete checkpoints by supplying a few quick feedback notes, through peer or student-teacher conferencing, or by using Google Docs tools.

FIGURE 6.5

Actionable Feedback Stems

Clarity

- Your description of _____ was easy to picture/follow because _____.
- Your use of (color, spacing, symbols, etc.) added clarity because _____.
- We understood this part _____, but _____.
- We weren't sure what you meant by _____. Did you mean _____?
- We were confused by this wording: _____. Maybe you can say it this way: _____.
- Can you say more about/provide examples of/add a quote to support _____?

Form/Format

- All parts have been completed.
- The format for _____ is correct and complete.
- This part _____ seems to be missing. Try checking with this resource/example _____ to get ideas.

Planning/Researching/Constructing

- Your plan was thorough. All parts were completed.
- The investigation design was effective in the following ways: _____. It led to successful completion of _____.
- It looks like (step 3, citations, etc.) is missing. Do you want some help with this part?

Accuracy

- The facts/terms/diagrams are accurate and compelling because _____.
- You might want to fact-check this point _____ because we think _____. Try using this source: _____.
- Your interpretations of _____ lack supporting evidence.
- We think you missed this problem-solving step because _____.

Impact

- This was an interesting/surprising idea _____.
- We agree/disagree with your solution/conclusions because _____.
- I think our perspective is different from yours because _____. Did you consider this (e.g., data, limitation) _____?
- So, do you recommend or think this _____?

Favorite No/Favorite Yes. "My Favorite No" is a popular and effective error-analysis strategy that comes from the Teaching Channel (see "Related Resources"). In the video, the teacher gives a short pre-assessment task, collects the work (in this lesson, the work is on index cards), and quickly sorts the cards into two piles—"yes" or "no." "No" means that something is done incorrectly, but something good may also be evident in the work. "Yes" means there are no errors. The teacher selects one example for class analysis from the "no" pile, copying the response and making the work anonymous. First, students collaboratively analyze the response and explain what the student did do correctly. With each explanation, the teacher probes for a rationale (for example, "How do we know the student distributed? What does it mean to *distribute*? Why is this step important?"). They identify all correct areas of the problem *before* discussing any missteps. Again, the teacher uses probing questions to uncover why an answer is or isn't correct ("How do you know? Can someone convince me?"). Many teachers I've worked with also use the reverse of this strategy, selecting an excellent "yes" problem for students to examine why it is done so well. Students can also create their favorite yes/no examples for other groups to analyze. The groups have to decide if the example is a "yes" (good example) or "no" (poor example), and then explain why.

Reflective Journaling. With Reflective Journaling, learners practice uncovering their own thinking. This differs from taking notes and simply listing information, which many students do without considering *why* they wrote something down. A reflection can communicate how a learner is or isn't making sense of the content. Students can describe things that confuse them, using sketchnotes to connect ideas, or explain their rationales for decisions they made during product development. At the end of a project, students can draw on their entries that have captured their thinking in the moment to create a reflective essay. Be sure to remind students to date each entry in case they want to reference it later on.

Reflective Journaling provides ongoing feedback opportunities between a student and teacher and is a viable alternative to face-to-face conferencing. When using reflective journals, establish how, when, or if journal entries will be shared with others. These are not assignments for the teacher to grade. The student might use a signal—such as a sticky note with a question on a particular page of the journal—to let the teacher know when they want to share a reflection or get feedback or support. The Facing History and Ourselves website is an excellent resource for introducing students to Reflective Journaling; it features a range of journal prompts for self-reflection and for reflecting on media, life, and acts of kindness.

Stages 4 and 5. Interpret evidence and frame feedback; determine next steps to advance learning.

John Hattie's research (2012) identified the effect of timely feedback (effect size = 0.75) to be much greater than an expected year's achievement (0.40). According to Hattie, feedback is most effective when students do not have proficiency or mastery. Thus, feedback thrives with incomplete knowing and understanding. Errors invite opportunities to learn—and both teachers and learners should embrace them.

To provide timely, meaningful feedback, first determine what information will be immediately useful to the learner. For example, in a writing conference, a student might need to address several areas to improve the first draft; however, listing everything that a student needs to correct is not as useful as suggesting *the first thing* to work on. A teacher from Delaware shared with me one of his strategies: He gave his students the opportunity to determine which of their drafts might benefit from feedback and which ones might not. During the week, students drafted three different pieces of writing. At the end of the week, they chose one of the drafts to hand in for feedback; they kept one draft to continue working on and tossed out the third because they thought it wasn't ever going to get any better.

Actionable feedback helps students know where they are along the learning trajectory, where they need to go next, and which tiny steps are likely to get them moving in the right direction. Several strategies we have discussed support metacognition and reflection. Metacognitive Task Cards, 5-Minute Teacher–Student Writing Conferences, and the 20-Minute Peer Feedback System (see Chapter 2) encourage students to identify what they are doing and why they are doing it. Discussions and feedback from teachers or peers help learners set their next goals for learning. Collaborative Inquiry Planning (Chapter 3) reinforces goal setting, planning, and team self-assessment using success criteria. Carousel Feedback (Chapter 4) teaches students to use reasoning to critique and give feedback to peers. With the Six-Word Memoir (Chapter 5), learners reflect on who they are as a person and learner and present their stories visually. All these feedback and reflection strategies are useful in driving engagement and learning forward.

Stage 6. Use performance tasks to assess transfer and deepen learning.

Two strategies for giving feedback lend themselves well to complex projects and longer investigations: Scrum Boards and Gallery Walks.

Scrum Boards. In Chapter 4, the scrum board served as a management tool to scaffold complex, multiday projects from start to finish (for example, with headings such as "To Do," "Doing," and "Done"). Peer review and feedback are built into the scrum board process when groups are assigned to provide feedback to another team as each task is completed. Scrum boards enable teachers to simultaneously oversee the progress of all teams while providing targeted support and feedback to individual teams when needed. Scrum boards build peer feedback into the *processes* of projects.

Gallery Walks. Gallery walks use peer feedback to critique *final products*. Before the gallery walk begins, each team prepares a short presentation of their work, which can include a poster display, podcast, or short video describing their final products (for example, how they built a scale model). Digital screencasting tools (such as Screencast-O-Matic or Screenr) work well for recording short presentations and posting to a digital portfolio or class web page.

Each team takes six to eight minutes to review another team's display, discuss what feedback they'll give, and record their comments before moving on. Gallery walk displays can take place in hallways or along the outside walls of a school building or be posted digitally for viewing and commenting. To maintain the efficient flow of movement, provide a feedback sheet that targets specific qualities of the final product (aligned with scoring rubrics), along with sample feedback stems. (See Appendix A for a student and peer assessment checklist for gallery walks.) Each team receives at least two critiques from classmates and then reviews and reflects on what they've heard. A whole-class discussion before and after the gallery walk is an excellent way to promote respectful peer critiquing in improving the quality of future projects and the quality of student interactions.

When you introduce Gallery Walks to your students for the first time, use products they can develop in one or two class periods, such as a bumper sticker with a math meme; a "Who Am I?" wanted poster of a famous person (which features just a silhouette with clues); or a "one-pager" about a poem, movie, or historical event. Students leave short feedback "tickets" at each display with three comments: one thing we learned, what we liked best and why, and one question or suggestion we have.

Student-Led Conferences. Many schools have used student-led conferences; however, in most schools, student self-reflection has rarely become an integral part of the school's systematic assessment and reporting practices. But there are ways to structure such conferences so that they highlight student self-reflection: In parent conferences, students can choose work samples they want to share to show their progress, and in conferences with teachers, students can discuss work samples to collaboratively evaluate for the purposes of grading and goal setting.

Ron Berger, senior advisor for teaching and learning at EL Education, describes student-led parent conferences as an engine that can transform teacher practice, increase parent engagement, and build metacognitive skills in students at any grade level (see "Related Resources"). Students select work that demonstrates something they have mastered and something they're still working on, based on their learning targets. They can identify something they are proud of as well as something they still need help with. Equally important, students reflect on their academic and personal goals, as well as on the learning that has been most meaningful to them. Metacognitive phrases and sentence starters can help students plan how they will articulate what they want to share:

A piece of work I'd like to share with you is _____ because _____.

One thing I struggled with was _____.

Here's what I learned in creating this piece.

This is how I think I grew as a learner from doing this.

A second student-led conferencing model that I've had the opportunity to observe firsthand is the Concord Regional Technical Center (CRTC) Student Performance upon Understanding Review (SPUR) (see "Related Resources"). First implemented during the 2008–2009 school year, the SPUR process has a simple premise: Being successful in a career and technical center must correlate to being successful in the working world. SPUR conferences, which take place four times each year, combine a job performance review with a school report card. Students must complete a self-evaluation of their work before meeting privately with teachers to discuss their performance using competency-based rubrics. Competencies define the "big" theoretical understandings and practical and technical skills required for a career, whether it's in the field of construction, health sciences, or graphic arts, as well as the personal and interpersonal qualities that employers value, such as professionalism, teamwork, leadership, and perseverance.

Competency-based rubrics structure teacher and student expectations during SPUR meetings. They are crucial to the success of the SPUR process and are one area of focus for my professional development work with the CRTC staff over the years. Early in the semester, teachers review the rubrics with students and have them rewrite the performance indicators in their own words so students clearly understand how to demonstrate evidence of learning.

Figure 6.6 illustrates the technical skills section of a rubric designed by CRTC automotive technology instructors Jesse Gregoire and Scott Mayotte. In all courses at this career and technical center, rubrics define performance in terms of increasingly complex careers, using DOK level skills. As students work through each course, they must provide the evidence that is listed under each performance level—in the form of assignments and assessments—making it clear that a student can do well on a lower-level skill (setting up the digital multimeter) but will still need to show evidence of learning at deeper levels to be considered proficient overall.

Course assessment data and work samples for each student are stored in individual CRTC Evidence Portfolios. To prepare for each conference, students select work they want to

FIGURE 6.6

Competency-Based Rubric for Student-Led SPUR Conferences

Course: Automotive Technology Program

Instructors: Jesse Gregoire and Scott Mayotte

Competency: Electrical/Electronic Systems: Understand the procedures and techniques of electrical/electronic systems in order to repair and maintain them.

School: Concord Regional Technical Center, New Hampshire

	Expanding (DOK 4) Routinely extend thinking and work beyond a proficient level.	**Proficient (DOK 3)** Analyze, research, and apply knowledge and skills to solve typical industry problems.	**Developing (DOK 2)** Know and show how system components align and work together.	**Beginning (DOK 1)** Recall, remember, and categorize routine details related to industry systems.
CTE DOK Performance Description				
Occupational Pathways	**A Technician: Shop Foreman**	**A Technician**	**B Technician**	**C Technician/ Lube Technician**
Practice/ Technical Skills **Performance Indicators**	I can . . . Make recommendations and repairs based on conclusions from the voltage drop test results. Make recommendations and repairs based on conclusions from the resistance test results. Make recommendations and repairs based on conclusions from test results. Maintain, restore, reinitialize, or code electrical systems.	I can . . . Make conclusions of circuit performance based on voltage and voltage drop test results. Make conclusions of circuit performance based on resistance test results. Make conclusions of circuit performance based on test results.	I can . . . Measure voltage and voltage drop. Measure resistance. Measure current. Remove, replace, and reinstall electrical components.	I can . . . Set up the digital multimeter. Inspect and clean electrical system components. Verify electrical system operation.
Evidence	**Manufacture Certification:** Electrical Systems Certification **ASE Student Certification:** Electrical/Electronic Systems	**CRTC:** Basic Electrical Test **Manufacture Certification:** Electrical Systems Certification **ASE Student Certification:** Electrical/ Electronic Systems	**CRTC:** Basic Electrical Test	**CRTC:** Basic Electrical Test

Source: Rubric for Student-Led SPUR Conferences, by J. Gregoire and S. Mayotte, Concord Regional Technical Center. Reprinted with permission.

highlight for discussion using preparation tools and the guidance provided. When students meet with instructors, they use rubrics and their evidence to self-assess their progress, get teacher feedback, and "negotiate" agreement on final performance ratings. Together, they review previous goals and establish new ones for the next semester.

SPUR conversations begin with a short teacher prompt; students do most of the talking while the teacher listens. Only then do teachers ask students a series of probing questions to help them evaluate and defend their work using solid examples of evidence that matches rubric descriptors. Teachers told me it took them a long time to learn how to do more listening than talking during SPUR conferences; when they let students talk, student-led conferences became a true learning experience for both teachers and students.

Regardless of the approach taken, Berger cautions that the first year implementing student-led conferences (SLCs) will be challenging. Students and parents will not fully understand their value and purpose, and teachers will probably underestimate the planning and supports needed for students to learn how to lead the discussions. Many schools that have put in the effort to implement SLCs agree that this practice has transformed school culture and created equity in the system.

Portfolio Defense. Some school districts use portfolio defenses as an alternative to grading extended projects (such as capstones, community service projects, and independent investigations) or administering end-of-year exams. (See "Related Resources" to view a video produced by Envision Learning Partners of what Portfolio Defense can include.) The philosophy underlying a public portfolio defense is that *self-reflection is the assessment*, demonstrating transfer of learning within an authentic context. Students can reflect on their growth over time using what is known as a *learning portfolio*. For example, they might demonstrate improvement in their math problem-solving skills using video clips and student work samples from different times in the school year. Or students can choose examples of their best work to showcase, such as a curated collection of high-quality art products they've created or evidence of how they successfully managed a complex project from start to finish.

Portfolio defenses are not limited to individual projects. They are also suitable for group projects, with group members presenting what they learned specific to their individual contributions. The quality of final group products might receive a "group" rating, much like in the Olympics when individual members from a gymnastics or ice skating team contribute to an overall team score.

Students use guidelines and the rubrics provided to select evidence from a body of work completed over time to highlight how they have met several related competencies. Defense rationales often include evidence of the research processes the students have engaged in and the decisions they've made along the way, as well as how their final product connects to a specific driving or essential question. Students formally present and defend what they've learned to a panel, which may include students (possibly one from each grade level) and adults (teachers, community members, or business and industry professionals). Before the portfolio defense, panel members meet to discuss expectations and how they will interpret rubric descriptors; by doing so, they calibrate their agreed-on ratings to reflect valid and reliable feedback to students. Panel members often use multiple rubrics or criteria to evaluate the evidence presented. This latter is often multifaceted because it comprises products, processes, feedback from mentors, and more. (See Appendix B, "Teacher Tools," for sample prompts using BEST Self-Direction, Collaboration, and Creative Thinking rubrics to guide student-led conferences or portfolio defenses.)

To Sum Up

Figure 6.7 summarizes some of the ways you might apply the metacognitive and reflection strategies described in this and earlier chapters to deepen understanding and engagement. Many of these strategies target multiday performance assessments and projects, whereas others you can embed in a single lesson.

Now that we have looked at all five essential teacher moves, it's time we considered how to put all of this together—the topic of our final chapter.

RELATED RESOURCES

- **The 20-Minute Peer Feedback System**
  www.spencerauthor.com/the-20-minute-peer-feedback-system

- **BEST Toolkits**
  www.best-future.org/resources

- **Facing History and Ourselves: Reflective Journals**
  www.facinghistory.org/ela/coming-age/unit-planning-toolkit/teach-facing-history-journal-prompts

- **"My Favorite No: Learning from Mistakes" (video)**
  https://learn.teachingchannel.com/video/class-warm-up-routine

- **Peer Feedback (Using Rubric Success Criteria)**
  www.karin-hess.com/learning-progressions

- **Portfolio Defense**
  www.envisionlearning.org/portfolio-defense

- **"Show & Tell: New Thinking About Student Engagement" (video)**
  www.ascd.org/el/articles/show-and-tell-a-video-column-new-thinking-about-student-engagement

- **SPUR Assessment Process**
  www.thecrtc.org/spur-assessment

- **SPUR Sample Conference Video**
  www.youtube.com/watch?v=ueRcBg8uYS8

- **Student-Led Conferences: Kindergarten**
  www.youtube.com/watch?v=dmIReiqI1ec

- **Student-Led Conferences: Kindergarten with Parents**
  www.youtube.com/watch?v=xvsHi1sZf9U

- **Student-Led Conferences Podcast**
  www.hthunboxed.org/tag/slc-miniseries

- **Student-Led Conferences: A How-to Guide (video)**
  www.hthunboxed.org/unboxed_posts/student-led-conferences-a-how-to-guide

- **Virtual Portfolio Defense Toolkit Developed by Envision Learning Partners**
  www.hewlett.org/wp-content/uploads/2020/10/ELPVirtualDefenseToolkitcc3.0.pdf

FIGURE 6.7

Actionable Strategies for Tasks That Use Reflection to Transfer Learning

Actionable Assessment Cycle Stages	Strategies	Primary Purpose	Look Fors: Students use metacognition and reflection to . . .
1. Clarify learning targets.	Essential Questions	Frame a unit of study or plan a lesson focus.	Explain new learning or new insights related to the essential or driving question.
	Driving Questions	Launch project-based learning.	
2. Embed short-cycle formative tasks into instruction.	Roll the Dice	Practice giving targeted feedback to peers.	Give targeted feedback to peers.
	Feedback Stems	Practice giving feedback using descriptive language.	
	Metacognitive Bookmarks	Practice using strategies that aid comprehension.	Compose running notes to annotate texts or write reflection entries.

Actionable Assessment Cycle Stages	Strategies	Primary Purpose	Look Fors: Students use metacognition and reflection to . . .
3. Uncover thinking and document evidence of learning.	Interactive Checkpoints	Break larger tasks into smaller parts to get feedback at each checkpoint during a project or longer performance-based assessment.	Give targeted feedback to peers.
	Favorite No/Favorite Yes	Collaboratively analyze solutions or explanations to locate and explain how and why to correct mistakes.	
	Reflective Journaling	Use prompts to guide "quick writes" to capture ongoing thinking or decision making during a project.	Document personal connections with new learning.
4. Interpret evidence and frame feedback. *and* **5. Determine next steps to advance learning.**	Metacognitive Task Cards	Short metacognitive prompts for self or peers.	Use prompts for group discussions and written reflections.
	5-Minute Teacher–Student Writing Conferences	Self-reflection, self-assessment, goal setting.	Analyze work products, seek feedback, and refine work quality; set goals based on progress.
	20-Minute Peer Feedback System	Peers form partner groups to give and receive feedback.	
	Collaborative Inquiry Planning	Peer goal setting and planning; self-assessment using success criteria.	Develop a plan to guide investigations.
	Carousel Feedback	Peer feedback or critique; developing reasoning skills.	Apply reasoning skills; develop evidence-based arguments.
	Six-Word Memoir	Shorter video project introducing self as a learner.	Visually represent interpretations of complex ideas.
6. Use performance tasks to assess transfer and deepen learning.	Gallery Walks	Peers cycle from group to group, providing feedback and critiques.	Support reasoning through collaborative discourse, supplying evidence at the end of a project.
	Scrum Boards	Team management tool tracks progress; peer feedback and critique are required after each item is completed.	Monitor multiple tasks during projects; provide peer feedback using criteria.
	What's My Story?	Video project for personally meaningful learning.	Investigate open-ended questions of personal interest; use media to share learning.

(continued)

FIGURE 6.7

Actionable Strategies for Tasks That Use Reflection to Transfer Learning (*continued*)

Actionable Assessment Cycle Stages	Strategies	Primary Purpose	Look Fors: Students use metacognition and reflection to . . .
6. Use performance tasks to assess transfer and deepen learning. (*continued*)	Student-Led Conferences	Students select work samples and discuss learning, using rubrics and guidance provided.	Analyze work products, seek feedback, and refine work quality; set learning goals based on progress.
	Portfolio Defenses	Students prepare, present, and defend what they learned, using work samples, rubrics, and guidance provided.	Provide a rationale for meeting learning expectations using work samples and self-reflections.

7

Putting It All Together— By Design, Not Chance

To enact deeper teaching, the teacher needs to make a myriad of decisions—some while plan-
ning a class and others on the spot, while teaching that class—about what content to teach,
how to build on students' current understanding of it, how to engage them in talking about
that content in public, how to show them that there's no shame in getting the wrong answer,
how to convince them that they can and will learn material that now seems to lie beyond
their abilities, how to design activities that will get pairs and groups of students to work
together productively, and so on. Deeper teaching is enormously complicated, and it is and
always has been rare in U.S. classrooms. So, then, how can large numbers of teachers learn to
manage this kind of complexity and provide this sort of instruction on a regular basis?

—Magdalene Lampert, "Deeper Teaching," in Jobs for the Future,
An Introduction to the Deeper Learning Research Series

Educators always appreciate having practical, easy-to-implement strategies; many excellent
ones are included in each chapter of this book. If we don't use *rigorous* strategies to build
a coherent system, however, they become a collection of things a teacher might do on any
given day—by chance, rather than by design.

Several years ago, I was working with 1st grade teachers who had created choice boards
called "The Nifty 9." They were set up like tic-tac-toe boards, with nine activities that students could choose from at different times during the day. Students loved the choice boards.
Teachers loved them, too. I loved the idea of choice boards—but I didn't love the choices they
were giving their students. When we began our workshop on depth of knowledge, I asked

teachers to analyze the choice board activities in terms of intended DOK levels. Within minutes, there was a collective "aha" in the room. All of the choices were low-level fun and engaging activities that didn't require much thinking. The focus was on emotional engagement without deeper cognitive engagement. Rigorous activities can tap personal connections leading to cognitive engagement. For example, students enjoyed drawing a picture to go with a book they had read; asking them to draw a picture of the most interesting part and explaining why it was interesting would have uncovered their thinking. Completing math problems and then using a code for the answers to color in a picture (for example, 14 = red, 10 = blue) was fun; creating five of their own problems, all having the answer of 14 could stretch their thinking. It's no wonder that when we suddenly ask students to think deeply after they have been happily drifting down a lazy stream, it's as if we have thrown them into rapid waters without the skills they need to stay afloat. If you've ever gone whitewater rafting, you know that with the right guide, the right preparation, and the right equipment, the experience can be both challenging and exhilarating.

Sadly, I still see many choice boards, even at the high school level, that keep students busy without asking for much of a learning stretch. The good news? It wasn't hard for those 1st grade teachers to revise their choice board activities once they understood how and why to do it.

My caution, then, is that you can use turn-and-talk strategies, small-group activities, choice boards, and stations that only focus on basic concepts and skills. You can implement project-based learning and independent investigation activities that are, for the most part, teacher-designed and teacher-directed, with little or no student decision making or input to personalize the learning. You can easily implement "learning lite" and call it rigorous—or, if you choose, strive for "learning deep."

The focus of this chapter is to weave together the five essential teacher moves to achieve the greatest effect of rigor on student-driven learning, instructional and assessment planning, and implementation across the school system. Implementing rigor by design means *there are no more random acts of rigor!*

The Student Perspective on Rigor by Design: A Focus on Rigorous Expectations

In schools that focus on rigorous learning, everyone in the school community understands the expectations and knows how the school will support students in achieving them. Teachers collaborate with colleagues to define deep learning and develop a shared understanding of expectations across subject areas, classrooms, and grade levels. Standards-based and competency-based grading evaluate what students know and can do—not in relation to various teachers' subjective criteria but in relation to established expectations. Students collaborate with peers to develop a shared understanding of what "good enough" looks like by codeveloping authentic products, critiquing one another's work, and self-assessing personal progress.

To make transparent your high expectations for learning, teach students how their brains process information (the "handy" brain model) so that they become more aware of and regularly monitor their engagement during learning. In addition, consistently use classroom discourse and student-generated questions to uncover thinking and deepen understanding. Discourse strengthens skills needed for respectful face-to-face conversations, increases engagement, and encourages students to think aloud, sharing their reasoning as well as clarifying misconceptions.

But two other skills are essential. In rigorous classrooms, students understand how to use self-reflection skills to capitalize on mistakes, and they are able to—and encouraged to—design their own complex tasks. Let's look at each of these in turn.

Using Reflection to Learn from Mistakes

What does the phrase "learning from your mistakes" really mean? And how can we help students do this when all mistakes are not created equal? Learning expert Eduardo Briceño (2015) identifies four types of mistakes and explains what we can learn from each one of them.

The sloppy mistake. We make sloppy mistakes when we're doing something we already know how to do, but we do it incorrectly because we lose our concentration. What can we learn from making too many sloppy mistakes? That we need new strategies to enhance our focus or build stamina during learning. Simply telling learners to take their time or check their work has rarely been effective in reducing sloppy mistakes. Students who understand *why* they need a concrete strategy to help them focus might be more willing to practice using it and reflecting on its effectiveness. Suggesting several strategies for students to choose from—such as an interactive checklist—gives them ownership of the strategies they decide to use.

The high-stakes mistake. We try to avoid making these mistakes because the result could be catastrophic (for example, taking risks while driving) or because making too many mistakes on a required exam could affect our future plans (for example, getting into college, passing a course, becoming licensed). Making mistakes like these has consequences. The best way to learn from making too many high-stakes mistakes is to invest more time and effort into *preparation*. For example, peers can study together or build in checkpoints to determine when they are ready for a high-stakes assessment.

The "aha" moment—a random and positive mistake. These can occur when something we did not intend to do leads to new learning (for example, making a mistake in a recipe that improves the meal); when we achieve our goal in an unexpected way, perhaps by taking a risk because we lacked the knowledge or skills needed to complete a challenging task; or when data prove to us that something we've been doing over and over just won't work. The best way to learn from aha moments is to reflect on why things worked out the way they did or examine the data that help us see a situation differently (for example, by analyzing a presentation recorded on video). When students have aha moments, they can ask themselves, *What are the data telling me? What caused that result to occur?* In the absence of doing so, applying new learning to future situations will remain random and infrequent at best.

The stretch mistake—the best type of mistake to learn from. Stretch mistakes happen when you take a risk and make some errors while trying to expand your current abilities. If we never made stretch mistakes, we'd never really challenge ourselves to acquire new knowledge and skills. Stretch mistakes place value on risk taking—and that's what rigorous tasks should do. If we keep making mistakes of this sort, we might need to slow down to complete the task, use a different strategy, or adjust the task itself, keeping it beyond what we can easily accomplish but incrementally adding different elements to the challenge as we master each part. The learning remains within our zone of proximal development while still moving forward. Students first need to believe that stretch mistakes have value—that they did some good thinking or made progress, although they have not yet found the final solution. Calling these mistakes by name—stretch mistakes—promotes risk taking and a growth mindset, suggesting that success is possible.

Help students analyze their stretch mistakes in relation to the learning goal and success criteria (much like the Favorite No/Favorite Yes activity). Have peer groups identify what they learned from the stretch mistake and generate ways to adjust their approach, such as by breaking down the task into smaller parts. These analyses can be part of reflection activities when groups or individuals are working on extended projects or preparing for student-led conferences.

Student-Designed Complex Tasks

Although many teachers might like the idea of students designing some of their own learning tasks, few want to take the risk. Several questions arise: *How will I manage too many tasks going in different directions at the same time? What if students don't stay on task? What if their ideas of a rigorous task are not the same as mine? And how can I get through everything I need to teach if my students are focusing on something else?* These are important questions to address and resolve.

To illustrate what this process looks like in practice, I'd like to share how one middle school teacher managed the process the first time she asked her students to design their own rigorous tasks. In early 2021, I received an email from Brenda Favila, a 7th grade English and Advanced Learning Lab teacher in the Alpine School District in Utah. The subject line read, "Student-friendly handout for DOK?" This, of course, intrigued me. Brenda had been using my DOK tools to design learning tasks for her classes and wanted to introduce the DOK levels to the 7th graders in her Advanced Learning Lab class. She wanted her students to use a variety of DOK levels in designing the group activities they were going to complete for books they had read. Her email closed with, "I was thinking this would be super cool for them to try."

Later that day, I sent her my Project Planning by DOK Level tool developed exactly for this purpose. (See Appendix A, "Student-Friendly Tools.") This tool is a trimmed-down version of the Hess Cognitive Rigor Matrix tools, with room for students to fill in the kinds of activities they are planning at each DOK level. After Brenda shared the tool with her students, she wrote to tell me what one of her 7th grade boys said when she asked them to explain what the phrase *cognitive rigor matrix* meant: "It's Dr. Hess's *mental effort chart*." "Yes!" she replied, smiling.

At this time, some of Brenda's students were learning remotely, so she broke the tool down into a series of slides to use with online group discussions. The first session was an overview that looked at how each DOK level differed from the others. In the following session, small groups started planning an activity that required using multiple DOK levels and creating "I can" statements.

After several days, I checked back with Brenda to see how the planning was going. She valued the fact that the tool enabled students to confirm that they were, indeed, mixing in different DOK levels in creating a group activity. The goal of the project was to create an 8- to 10-minute learning activity based on a theme from two books the class read; they could focus on common elements from both books or just focus on one book. The activity had to have three different DOK element levels of their choice, and the students labeled what level they thought they were addressing on the DOK planning page. This framework was helpful because it enabled them to create a more engaging activity by purposefully incorporating different DOK levels. The planning took two class periods; the presentations were on a third day. Noted Brenda, "This also helped my students see a connection to different [DOK] levels they experience in all their classes that they might not have realized were there before." Now *I* smiled. Yes!

Brenda and her students proved that you can still teach the content you're required to teach—read two novels—and engage students in task design, that students can design meaningful learning activities when given structure (tools, time to engage with peers) and teacher support, and that it's best to take it slowly at first. Brenda's students were integrating new knowledge about DOK with something they had done in the past—reading and analyzing novels. The next time, students will already have a working knowledge of DOK and how to design a task with multiple DOK levels. They also will have seen—and learned from—the different ways their peers designed tasks for this unit of study.

And along the way, they will have experienced productive struggle—and sometimes productive failure. This serves two crucial cognitive functions: It activates prior knowledge and encourages students to explore an array of possible solutions to novel, complex problems that the teacher may not have taught (Jackson, 2021). With productive failure, "success occurs after students reach an impasse (or a standstill) during a learning experience.... Delaying direct instruction assists with the development of problem-solving skills, helping students discern information for future learning situations" (Jackson, 2021, pp. 1–2).

Brenda gave her students a novel, complex assignment, trusting them to productively struggle with their peers to design new learning tasks for themselves. Observing the struggles students face while solving complex problems provides insights into when explicit instruction is warranted.

My only regret? I wish I'd suggested to Brenda that she ask her students to reflect on designing their own learning activities. That was a missed opportunity for learning on my part. I have no doubt that Brenda and her students are risk takers, and they likely made some stretch mistakes and had some aha moments along the way.

The Teacher Perspective on Rigor by Design: A Focus on Lesson and Assessment Planning

Not every well-planned lesson necessarily leads to deeper thinking and understanding. Take, for example, a lesson that begins with the teacher identifying the learning target, aligned with a grade-level standard. The lesson might have a focus question, with a KWHL activity to activate prior knowledge. The teacher uses a related entry point from the discussion to begin instruction, defines and models a given skill or strategy, and asks students to practice with a partner. The teacher observes, provides targeted feedback, and then gives an assignment for independent practice or assigns students to different stations, where they practice and apply the new strategy in different ways.

This was a well-designed lesson, but it didn't stretch student thinking. From this scenario, we don't know what the teacher planned for the rest of the week. So we're left wondering: Is a broad essential or driving question sparking an investigation using today's new skill? Will students tackle authentic real-world problem-solving tasks that increase with complexity throughout the unit of study? Will small groups generate some of their own ideas for how to integrate the new skill with other skills they've already mastered? What will the evidence of student learning look like? Will there be opportunities for peer feedback or self-reflection in addition to teacher-made tests and assignments?

The goal of rigorous lesson and unit design is to actively engage students in meaningful learning that offers choice and decision making about how students demonstrate knowledge of the "bigger ideas" they've acquired through the processes they've used and the products they've created. Although there is a time and place for direct instruction, it shouldn't be the only way to support learning. And as the research (Jackson, 2021) suggests, sometimes withholding direct instruction while students wrestle with a complex task promotes deeper levels of learning.

Seeing the Forest for the Trees

Tan Huynh (2022) uses the metaphor of forests, trees, and leaves to describe his lesson-planning process for multilingual learners. The forest represents the global view of the intended learning—the processes students will use to learn content, resulting in products demonstrating their learning. I would also add an open-ended essential question to the forest "level" of unit planning, providing the "global why" for the learning—the forest canopy. When students can envision how they will transfer the processes and content learned to create products demonstrating deeper learning, they begin to see the relevance of each day's lesson. As a reminder, content, processes, and products also embody the success criteria in the STARS planning model (situation, task, audience, roles and resources, success criteria) for designing performance assessments.

The lessons—or trees—collectively create the forest. These lessons can branch out in different ways, connecting topics and resources with investigations both teacher-guided and student-driven. Just as every tree is growing in the same forest, so every lesson drives learning toward applying processes to deepen content knowledge and create authentic products. Lessons can build background knowledge, connect new ideas with prior knowledge, or guide students to raise and investigate their own questions. Sometimes lessons focus on processes (how to take notes, how to collect data) or on how to develop a specific product (an infographic or a podcast). Each lesson has a learning target with a focus question that students should be able to answer by the end of a lesson (or series of lessons), helping them to connect today's learning with past learning and setting the stage for stretching their thinking in tomorrow's lessons.

Expanding on the forest–tree metaphor, the leaves represent the smallest grain size of lesson planning—the specific tasks students will complete to demonstrate the subskills needed for larger performance tasks. If one branch of the tree is research skills, the leaves on that branch might include developing a survey, conducting a key word search, and organizing a focus group. Teachers can teach these skills using direct instruction or offer them as choice activities with study guides at different stations. Sketchnoting a visual of trees with leaves that indicate related skills or tasks can help students see how their learning is connecting and building to become a larger body of learning—the forest.

Planning for Rigor

What, then, is the role of rigor in lesson design? *Rigor is the fertilizer that produces healthy, long-lasting learning—forests that flourish.* This fertilizer comes in the form of five essential nutrients—five teacher moves that collectively span every depth-of-knowledge level. When teachers employ the five moves in rigorous lesson and unit design, the goal of deepening learning for every student becomes achievable. As you plan instruction and assessment, consider how each lesson can build on prior learning to deepen thinking and broaden understanding.

Figure 7.1 superimposes two different kinds of tasks onto the Hess Cognitive Rigor Matrix template: short-cycle formative tasks and performance-based assessments. Combining these task types is essential to rigor-by-design planning. Short-cycle formative tasks build conceptual understanding and schemas, laying the groundwork for deeper learning. A range of performance-based assessments challenge students to transfer learning in new contexts.

Planning rigorous units and lessons does not have to be complicated. Use the preliminary planning template shown in Figure 7.2 to analyze a unit of study you currently teach or are planning to teach. Identify strategies you now use and skim the chapter summaries for others you might add to deepen the learning. Working with colleagues is a great way to explore the options.

FIGURE 7.1
Planning for Deeper Learning

Depth of Knowledge and Types of Thinking	DOK 1: Acquiring a Foundation	DOK 2: Using, Connecting, and Conceptualizing	DOK 3: Deepening and Constructing Meaning	DOK 4: Extending, Transferring, and Broadening Meaning
Remember	Short-Cycle Formative Tasks		Performance-Based Assessments	
Understand	• Ask probing questions of increasing complexity. • Build schemas. • Uncover thinking and document learning. • Scaffold learning. • Frame feedback. • Engage students in reflective and metacognitive thinking.		• Use open-ended contexts and broad questions inviting student-centered approaches. • Challenge current understandings. • Uncover thinking and document learning. • Require authentic doing and sharing. • Integrate academic and personal skills. • Transfer/apply prior learning in new contexts. • Engage students in reflective and metacognitive thinking.	
Apply				
Analyze				
Evaluate				
Create				

Let's now look at the steps you can take to plan a unit with rigor in mind:

- **Step 1.** Identify the content, processes, or skills in the unit of study or the project-based learning unit topic and develop at least one essential or driving question to frame the learning. Essential and driving questions are at DOK 3 or 4, creating multiple opportunities to transfer learning.

- **Step 2.** Skim the chapter summaries that describe each of the five teacher moves—ask probing questions, build schemas, strategically scaffold learning, design complex tasks, and engage students in metacognition and self-reflection. This may help you locate potential strategies for the unit. List possible strategies or activities in the middle column of Figure 7.2. Each teacher move will likely involve several of these. Add clarifying details. For example, if you list "stations," identify the content you will teach or reinforce at each station. If you don't already have performance-based assessments for this unit, you will need to either locate existing tasks or develop tasks with your colleagues. Check Appendices A and B for resources that might be useful.

- **Step 3.** Connect specific strategies or activities with learning targets. Matching learning targets ("I can" statements) with lesson activities establishes the sequence of lessons and the learning you're focusing on. Activities such as Fishbowl will take more

FIGURE 7.2
Embedding the Five Essential Teacher Moves

Essential Teacher Moves	Unit of Study or PBL:	Overarching Essential or Driving Question(s):
	List Potential Strategies	**Identify Learning Targets**
1. **Ask probing questions** (at any DOK level)		
2. **Build schemas** (DOK 2)		
3. **Strategically scaffold learning** (at any DOK level)		
4. **Design complex tasks** (DOK 3 and 4)		
5. **Engage students in metacognition and reflection** (at any DOK level) **Facilitate student self-reflections requiring supporting evidence** (DOK 3 and 4)		

than one class period to complete and may have more than one "I can" statement; for example, one statement might refer to preparation, one to providing supporting ideas, and one to posing questions to peers.

- **Step 4.** Create or locate materials to support each lesson. You might record short video guides for use in stations or locate video clips or visuals to build background knowledge.
- **Step 5.** Use the Rigor by Design Lesson and Unit Planning Template shown in Figure 7.3 to *briefly* describe the intended flow of learning. (See "Related Resources" for an interactive planning template.)

The School Perspective on Rigor by Design: A Focus on Teacher-Friendly Observation Supports

John Hattie's research (2009) identified that when teachers believe that their collective actions can positively influence student learning, higher overall student achievement results. According to Donohoo and Hite (2021),

> Lower expectations result in teachers assigning low-level tasks to students; this lowers students' own expectations about themselves. This diminished sense of efficacy results in students having a lack of willingness to take risks and apply new approaches. When low achievement is pervasive in a school, teachers can also start to feel *they* have less efficacy—individually and collectively. (p. 1)

I've created a walk-through tool, Looking for Rigor, for observing and documenting examples of student or teacher behaviors associated with deeper levels of thinking and learning (see Figure 7.4). Teachers can use the tool to observe their students or to observe in one another's classrooms, looking for specific behaviors (for example, do students persevere when given a challenge? Are they respectful when working with peers?). Coaches and school leaders can use the tool to see to what degree teachers have embedded specific strategies in their day-to-day practice. (See "Related Resources" for a link to the complete Looking for Rigor Observation Tool.)

Many schools I've worked with use the observation tool to collect baseline data when first starting to implement rigor by design. Schools tend to focus on one teacher move at a time, meeting as a faculty to discuss challenges and successes with each teacher move before expecting full implementation. Asking probing questions to uncover thinking is often the first teacher move that schools examine. Noticing the kinds of questions that students ask is generally a good indicator that the teacher has modeled probing questions.

FIGURE 7.3

Lesson and Unit Planning Template

DOK Levels and Focus	Teacher Roles: Planned Strategies	Planned Strategies for Unit: Observable Evidence of Learning	Student Roles: Observable Evidence of Learning	Observable Evidence of Learning in Unit
DOK Level 1. Acquire a foundation	• Questions focus attention (*Who? What? Where? How? When?*) • Directs, leads, demonstrates, defines • Monitors practice • Scaffolds for access and focus	*Teacher shows film clip of event; provides historical documents.* *Teacher question: What information can you find in each source that will help answer our inquiry-based question?*	• Acquires vocabulary, facts, rules, routines • Memorizes, recites, quotes, restates • Retrieves information, uses required tools and resources • Practices and self-monitors routine skills • Seeks support, asks questions to clarify procedures or task expectations	*Small groups read, take notes, and annotate various primary and secondary sources related to the topic or overarching question.*
DOK Level 2. Use, connect, and conceptualize	• Questions build schemas: differentiate parts from the whole, classify, explain relationships (*Can you explain examples/nonexamples? Cause/effect?*) • Draws out basic inferences • Models/scaffolds conceptual understanding (*Why? Under what conditions?*) • Provides guided practice for multistep tasks	*Teacher question: How does this information relate to what you've already found in other documents?* *Provide graphic organizer.* *Teacher question: Would making a timeline help?*	• Explains relationships, sorts, classifies, compares, organizes information, summarizes • Makes predictions based on estimates, observations, prior knowledge • Proposes problems, topics, or questions to investigate • Raises conceptual questions (*Why? What if?*) • Selects tool or strategy for specific purpose • Follows teacher-designed procedures	*Students organize notes using graphic organizers provided.* *Students summarize key ideas.*
DOK Level 3. Deepen and construct meaning	• Questions probe reasoning, thinking, planning (*How will you know or do this? Where is the evidence?*) • Promotes peer discourse and self-reflection to uncover big ideas, themes • Designs tasks requiring proof, justification, analysis of evidence quality, accuracy • Models/scaffolds validating sources • Supports student-designed performance tasks	*Teacher question: Is the source for this information credible?* *Teacher question: How can you check for credibility and accuracy? What should you look for if this is a print/nonprint source?* *Guide students to generate criteria for evaluating sources. Model an example.*	• Uncovers relevant, accurate, credible information, flaws in a design, or proposed solutions linked with big ideas, themes • Raises questions that explore underlying meanings (*Is that what the author is saying? What can we learn from this?*) • Plans how to develop supporting (hard) evidence for conclusions, solutions, claims • Researches, tests and revises ideas, solves nonroutine problems • Sets goals, monitors progress • Self-assesses, uses feedback to improve quality	*Students check for accuracy, credibility, and potential bias of sources provided.* *Students generate new questions.*
DOK Level 4. Extend, transfer, and broaden meaning	• Questions challenge or extend meaning (big ideas, themes), explore sources, broaden perspectives (*Are there potential biases? Can you propose an alternative model?*) • Models/scaffolds triangulating sources, peer-to-peer critique, self-reflection • Supports student-designed performance tasks • Promotes peer discourse and self-reflections to uncover big ideas, themes, trends	*Specific topic: Gulf of Tonkin incident* *Pose inquiry-based question before researching begins: Did this event cause the U.S. president to go to war with Viet Nam, or was the president already planning on doing that anyway?*	• Initiates, transfers, and constructs new knowledge; insights are linked to big ideas, themes • Modifies, creates, elaborates based on analysis and interpretation of multiple sources • Raises novel questions; investigates real-world problems and issues • Sets goals, monitors progress • Self-manages time and tasks • Generates self-reflections; self-assesses and uses feedback to improve work quality	*Students expand research and sources and triangulate information.* *Groups present findings from multiple sources to support their claims.*

Source: From Rigor by Design, Not Chance: Laying the Groundwork for Deeper Understanding (p.14), by K. Hess, 2018, Educational Research in Action. Adapted with permission.

FIGURE 7.4
Looking for Rigor Observation Tool

Teacher Behaviors	Student Behaviors

Teacher Move 1. Uses probing questions and adequate wait time to promote collaboration and discourse. Frames feedback or follow-up questions specific to student responses.
 	
Document specific teacher questions and questioning strategies observed:
 	
• Do the teacher's questions or strategies spark student questions?
• How does the teacher engage every student?
• Which questions ask for substantive conceptual or deep understanding?
	• Do students engage in substantive discourse about concepts, relationships, observations, predictions (if/then)?
	• Do they generate new questions that drive learning?
	  — Clarifying (DOK 1): *Where do we get the materials? When is this due?*
	  — Procedural (DOK 1 and 2): *What do we do next?*
	  — Conceptual (DOK 2): *Is this an example of _____? What would happen to the system if _____? Is this a pattern or trend?*
	  — Extending thinking (DOK 3–4): *Does this idea connect to the essential question? Where is there support for this claim/theory?*

Teacher Move 2. Provides accurate conceptual information and builds schemas. Frames feedback specific to concepts or deeper understanding. Document strategies/materials/resources used: • How does the teacher use modeling? (e.g., using think-alouds to show reasoning, using multiple modalities) • How does the teacher help students to see relationships (e.g., parts–whole, graphic organizer)?	• Do student responses go beyond memorized explanations, concepts, or theories? • Do students make connections, predictions, or observations to help them make sense of information? • Do students break down or analyze how parts work together to support the whole or identify missing parts?
Teacher Move 3. Monitors and scaffolds instruction to provide access and advance/deepen thinking. Frames feedback specific to moving students forward. Document strategies/materials/resources used to support access to tasks or complex material: • Did strategies match learning targets? • What did the teacher do to support their learning?	• Did students get stuck on anything? Did they persevere? What did they do: Seek help? Try something else? Start over? • Describe student engagement or the effectiveness of the scaffolding strategy used.
Teacher Move 4. Emphasizes deeper thinking, transfer, and productive struggle/challenge. Tasks require students to justify or support conclusions with reasoning. Frames feedback specific to each stage of complex tasks. Document prompts/materials/resources used: • Describe task students were working on or ask for a copy. • Describe student engagement.	• Did students have opportunities to make decisions about task design: content, processes, or products? • Did individuals or groups generate ideas or approaches to solving complex problems? • During group work, was every member involved and contributing? How did groups resolve their differences?
Teacher Move 5. Provides time during the lesson for every student to review, reflect on, and articulate what was learned. Both peer-to-peer reflection and self-reflection are valued. Frames feedback specific to student responses. Document prompts/materials/resources used: • What kind of reflection activities were used? • How frequently (every 10–15 minutes is suggested)? • Describe class norms/expectations for student engagement: respectful, using success criteria to critique, etc.	• Did students challenge one another respectfully and ask probing questions, providing their own evidence and qualifiers? • Did students show willingness to reflect and self-correct using feedback? • What did student engagement look like during peer-to-peer product development or peer critique activities? • Did peer feedback/self-reflection activities focus on quality (success criteria) and analyzing what to do next to improve?

When using the Looking for Rigor Observation Tool, be sure to document *the exact words* that teachers and students use, rather than paraphrasing what they say. This helps when collaboratively analyzing observations.

Before I use the tool in a given school, I ask teachers to observe and comment on teacher–student interactions using selected video clips in which teachers are clearly asking different types of questions and are scaffolding learning. Teachers work in pairs for this activity; one person focuses on the teacher; the other focuses on students. The look fors in the chapter summaries can be a helpful guide. Subsequent to watching the video, rich discussions ensue.

Once teachers fully understand how to document evidence during the walk-through, teams of two to three observers spend about 15 minutes together in the same classroom taking notes. One person focuses on the teacher, a second person focuses on students, and a third observer looks for connections, such as what students did when the teacher asked a question. Typically, after completing three classroom walk-throughs, the team meets to debrief. Team members can calibrate use of the tool and discuss ways to improve on making observations. If multiple observer teams are visiting different classrooms, they can meet together at the conclusion of the observations to debrief and look for trends across the school without singling out individual teachers. For example, they might pose any of the following questions: *What scaffolding strategies did we see today? Were they effective? Did both teachers and students generate substantive questions?* When I'm involved in the process, I like to share general trends with the entire faculty at the end of the day and identify a few exemplars that teachers observed. This provides evidence-based positive reinforcement that can encourage other teachers.

Remember that a walk-through only captures part of a larger lesson. Teachers will use different strategies at the beginning, middle, and end of any lesson. For example, building a schema generally happens earlier than guiding students as they engage with subsequent stages of complex performance tasks, such as conducting research or developing a final product.

Making Time for Rigor

Rome wasn't built in a day. Teachers will not be able to implement rigor by design quickly, either. Perhaps it's time to slow down and pay more attention to thinking about the concepts you're teaching in the curriculum rather than simply covering them.

We might take a page from the "slow education" playbook to reflect on our future vision of school. The slow education movement, founded by Maurice Holt in the United Kingdom, advocates for schools to give students time to engage in deep learning, explore what they're curious about, and reflect on their learning. Advocates of this approach oppose the use of high-stakes testing and rapid improvement initiatives in favor of spending more time developing collaborative cultures and supportive classroom relationships for learning. Slow education focuses on providing space for educators to work together and engage in the complex thinking needed to find more effective ways of educating hard-to-reach learners. To that end, Harris and colleagues (2017) point to the need for teachers and leaders

> to make time for deep consideration of complex matters, such as how to support the learning of every student within a school. Pressure for quick responses tends to lead to thinking that relies on what is already known. Put simply, we need to reduce the pressure on schools to allow people to engage in deeper, more creative thinking about these issues. (p. 3)

And I couldn't agree more.

RELATED RESOURCES

- **Better Lesson Teacher-Designed Lessons**
  https://teaching.betterlesson.com/search

- **CogKnow Software for Unit Planning**
  www.evolutionalliance.education/cogknow

- **Hess Lesson/Unit/Project Planning Template with DOK Levels**
  www.karin-hess.com/_files/ugd/5e86bd_2d6f90ffa4854ea983bb53970ec6133b.pdf

- **Hess Looking for Rigor Walk-Through Observation Tool**
  www.karin-hess.com/_files/ugd/5e86bd_d124d428960c47249e0ca87bc06acb59.pdf

Appendix A

Student-Friendly Tools

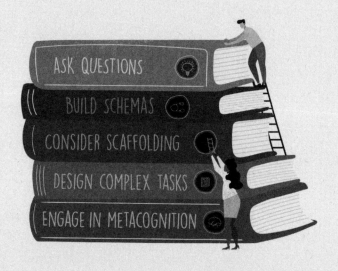

STUDENT TOOL 1

Student-Designed Investigations with Interactive Checkpoints

Investigators:			Date:
Title or Description of the Investigation:			Checkpoints
1. What is the testable question?	**What makes this a "testable" question?**		**OK to go on?**
Based on past observations or prior knowledge:			
Investigation Plan			**Feedback/Comments**
2. Hypothesis (predicts what will happen or change and what will cause the change)	**Variable to measure or observe**	**Variable(s) to control or keep the same**	
3. List equipment, materials, or technology needed (be specific—for example, two cups of water, a stopwatch, safety goggles)			
4. Describe the investigation step by step: safety procedures, number of trials, sample size, and so on. How will you control variables? Who is responsible for each task?			
5. Data display: How will you organize observations or measurements? • Data table or chart • Graph • Science journal or log • Labeled drawing • Photo, video • Other			
6. What did you learn? What are your conclusions? Do the data *support or refute* the hypothesis? Did you adapt or change any methods during the investigation? If so, explain why.			
7. Did the investigation raise any new questions or claims for a future investigation?			

Peer and Self-Assessment Checklist for Gallery Walks

Display Developers:

Reviewers: **Date:**

Investigation Components	What to Look For	👍	Notes/Feedback
Testable Question	• The question is clearly stated and can be answered using data from an investigation.		
Hypothesis	• A prediction is stated that can be tested using observations or investigation.		
Investigation Procedures	• The design (materials and procedures) matches the stated hypothesis. • The variables are clearly identified, noting which variables stay the same and what will be measured. • Procedures are clear enough so that others can replicate the investigation.		
Data Displays	• Data are well organized and accurate. • Data are clearly and accurately labeled using charts, tables, graphs, or diagrams.		
Analysis and Conclusions	• Analyses or conclusions relate to the testable question and hypothesis. • Conclusions are accurate and supported by the data analysis. • Specific data are used to support conclusions.		
New Questions or Claims	• A new question or claim is considered that can extend thinking and investigation.		

STUDENT TOOL 3
Writing Treatments and Developing Shooting Scripts

A **treatment** presents a summary of your story line, demonstration, or tutorial. This step organizes your ideas for a short video or longer documentary.

If you are making a tutorial video, ask your teacher for directions to plan a **Structured Minilesson.** Then use the following templates to plan your sequence of shots and how you will shoot the script.

Start by using index cards or sticky notes to identify your key ideas. After you've written about a dozen cards, move them around to determine the sequence and think about how to present the ideas visually.

Production Overview

Title: _____

I. Identify crew members for roles needed.

Director(s): _____

Script writer(s): _____

Researcher/fact checker: _____

Camera operator/cinematographer: _____

Film/video editor(s): _____

Equipment and materials manager: _____

Sound and lighting technician(s): _____

Other: _____

Target audience: _____

Narrative description (briefly describe the story line and purpose):

_____

_____

_____

_____

_____

_____

_____

_____

_____

_____

_____

II. Identify people "in front of" the camera.

Talent (who will take each part)	Describe role in the video (e.g., demonstrator, voiceover artist, on-camera performer)	Briefly describe each role

III. Identify general locations for each shoot.

#	Location(s) for the shoot; describe each setting	Talent and/or props needed?	Special techniques (e.g., camera, lighting)	Soundtrack/audio (e.g., music, sound effects)

IV. Use a spreadsheet to develop a storyboard and shooting script.

Shot #	Visuals	Audio (e.g., music, sound effects)	Voiceover/narration	Camera notes (e.g., long shot, close-up, pan)

STUDENT TOOL 4
Project Planning by DOK Level

Check skills you plan to use. Fill in notes regarding specific tools, terms, products, and so on. When completed, list evidence of successful completion.

DOK Levels	Student Roles and Tasks: I/we can . . .	Observable Evidence of My/Our Learning (with completion dates)
1. Acquire a Foundation	• Learn and use the following facts or vocabulary terms: _____ . • Retrieve/locate data or information (e.g., key word search, text search) . • Use tools (e.g., calculator, measurement), rules (e.g., editing), or specific resources. • Practice and self-monitor the following skills: _____ .	
2. Use, Connect, and Conceptualize	• Explain relationships (cause and effect, compare and contrast, if/then, parts-to-whole). • Organize information (e.g., outline, sketchnotes, mind map, graphic organizer) . • Summarize key steps, ideas, or events (e.g., storyboard, precis, podcast). • Make predictions based on observations, prior knowledge, and examples/nonexamples. • Propose questions (*Why? What if?*) or problems or topics to investigate. • Select and use tools or strategies for a specific purpose.	
3. Deepen and Construct Meaning	• Uncover relevant, accurate, and credible information; uncover flaws in a design or claims. • Identify links with big ideas or themes. • Raise questions that explore underlying meanings (*Is that what the author is really saying? What can we learn from this?*). • Plan how to develop supporting evidence for conclusions, solutions, or claims. • Research, test, and revise ideas; solve nonroutine problems. • Set learning goals and monitor my/our progress. • Self-assess; give or get feedback to improve quality (e.g., peer conference) .	
4. Extend, Transfer, and Broaden Meaning	• Construct new knowledge; link insights to big ideas or themes. • Modify, create, and elaborate based on analysis using multiple sources. • Raise novel questions *and* investigate real-world problems or issues. • Set learning goals and monitor progress (e.g., self-direction or collaboration) . • Self-manage my/our time on task. • Reflect on my progress/learning; self-assess and use feedback to improve quality.	

Problem-Solving Steps with Reasoning

The Problem/Scenario/Investigation:		
My Solution Path (the steps or investigation procedures I'll take, including developing representations, using materials or equipment)	**My Reasoning** (why this step works or makes sense)	**My Connections** (e.g., applying concepts, principles, theories, terms, symbols, models)

Appendix B

Teacher Tools

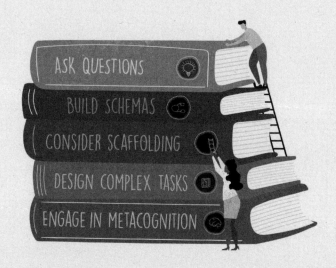

TEACHER TOOL 1
Scaffolding Strategies by DOK Levels

Matching Strategies to Learning Targets	Supporting Language and Vocabulary Development	Facilitating Executive Functioning; Applying Skills and Processes	Deepening Content Knowledge; Connecting to Big Ideas	Possible Student Activities or Products
DOK Level 1 **Acquire a Foundation**	• Use bilingual tools or apps to find definitions, synonyms, word families, and cognates. • Build **interactive Word Walls** with visuals (photos, drawings, symbols). • Build prior knowledge of content-specific vocabulary (tier 3 vocabulary) using different modalities and **word banks.**	• Post and clarify word meanings of daily "I can . . ." statements for specific skills to apply *today*. • Cocreate (color-coded) **anchor charts,** visually breaking down steps or parts. • **"Think aloud"** to model how to apply academic terms in each content area: list, define, brainstorm, locate, and follow steps or rules. • **Use structured note-taking** (two columns, visuals, concept maps).	• Build prior knowledge with **"Daily 10" Playlist, Wonder of the Day,** field trips, video, concrete objects, hands-on explorations, and skits or roles. • Create class tableaus for events, ideas, and concepts (e.g., division). • Use **KWHL** charts (H= How can we find out?) to lead into the lesson activities (e.g., read, build model). • Model or use **sketchnotes** to identify prior knowledge.	• Use different modalities (visuals, gestures, manipulatives, or word banks) to respond to basic questions. • Create personal picture dictionaries or glossaries. • Use frames and word banks to practice short responses: restate, describe, list. • Label photos and artifacts. • Teacher codevelops **anchor charts** and **paragraph frames** with students.
DOK Level 2 **Use, Connect, and Conceptualize**	• Model using word-solving strategies or patterns and context cues. • **"Think aloud"** to model how to do a key word search, **Picture Talk,** and **Wonder Walls.** • Move from definitional to conceptual, abstract, nonliteral, or multiple meanings (Tier 2 vocabulary). • Check understanding with **turn-and-talk frames** every 10–12 minutes. • Reinforce five new vocabulary words each day: repeat, use in context, define, connect the root meaning to similar words, and use in responses.	• Model how to apply academic terms in each content area (e.g., predict, compare, categorize examples and nonexamples, summarize, record or organize data). • Provide *customized* graphic organizers, tables, flowcharts, and software tools to organize ideas and data. • Break tasks into steps and checkpoints. • **Chunk text** and insert questions. • Use **Read-Draw-Write** and **Read-Draw-Do** to break down tasks.	• Preview texts before listening, viewing, or reading; discuss how to use text features (e.g., diagrams, visuals, subheadings, bold print). • Model the use of **graphic organizers, paragraph frames,** and **concept maps** for main idea and details, compare and contrast, cause and effect, and sequencing. • Use structured **Gallery Walks** to add or build on the ideas of others. • Model or use **sketchnotes** to build on prior knowledge.	• Peers build anchor charts for characters, events, and key concepts. • Use **anticipation guides** to predict and then check what the text says. • Make a cartoon strip showing the sequence of a process or story line (draw, cut out pictures). • Complete or create a timeline. • Organize information using a graphic organizer, concept map, or graph.

(continued)

TEACHER TOOL 1

Scaffolding Strategies by DOK Levels (continued)

Matching Strategies to Learning Targets	Supporting Language and Vocabulary Development	Facilitating Executive Functioning; Applying Skills and Processes	Deepening Content Knowledge; Connecting to Big Ideas	Possible Student Activities or Products
DOK Level 3 **Deepen and Construct Meaning**	• Use **TBEAR** (Topic or Thesis; Bridge to evidence or Brief summary; Evidence or Examples; Analyze examples; Reflect) to include supporting evidence. • Create TBEAR vocabulary posters. • Use anchor charts with **stems** for research or listening activities (e.g., This text says . . .; How does this compare?; This source doesn't agree with . . .; This fact or source is important or credible because . . .).	• Model how to apply academic terms in each content area; analyze by breaking into parts, use criteria, and find evidence. • Provide **hint cards** with definitions, bilingual cues, and illustrated examples to use when solving multistep problems or completing tasks. • Provide guided practice for whole-class and subsequent small-group performance tasks. • Regularly monitor progress using performance tasks while reducing scaffolding over time.	• Guide small groups to **co-develop inquiry plans** to investigate open-ended research questions or tasks. • Teach students to **annotate texts** (underline the key idea, circle key terms, and paraphrase each section). • Provide structured ways to reread texts for different purposes. • Use **Carousel Feedback** for peers to critique reasoning or solutions. • Provide guidelines for use of visuals.	• Use **anticipation guides** to gather evidence and reflect on initial ideas after reading. • Use **Fishbowl, Value Lines, Barometer,** and inner or outer circles to practice listening skills and to connect or support ideas. • Use **Jigsaw** for groups to take apart exemplars or models and teach peers. • Create a captioned photo essay for the topic, with given criteria or frames provided. • Complete **One-Pagers** to illustrate the meaning of a quote, a text, processes, or themes, for example.
DOK Level 4 **Extend, Transfer, and Broaden Meaning**	• Use pre-post **Word Splashes** to reinforce and integrate word meanings and concepts from sources across a unit or project. • Use video or audio recordings with check lists to **self-assess** and give **peer feedback.**	• Model or break down how to apply academic terms in each content area: analyze across sources or data sets, research, investigate, and check sources and credibility; complete first drafts, revising for clarity and flow of ideas. • Provide **graphic organizers** and models that encourage cross-text analyses. • Use a structured process or series of steps for multiple readings or viewing of texts or to self-assess task completion.	• Provide simulations (e.g., Hess **STARS** model), investigations, or debate formats to show varying perspectives or possible causes and effects. • Pair content-specific texts so that more basic print or nonprint texts provide background for a second text. • Use a structured process to **self-assess** content acquisition and understanding. • Use **Gallery Walks** and **Scrum Boards** for peers to critique projects.	• Small groups complete a **Media/Artifact Search** activity where an unknown visual or object is presented with a series of inquiry-based questions for students to answer (e.g., What event is depicted? When was this taken? Why is it significant? What sources did you check?). • Create a storyboard for video or dramatic production. • Offer student-driven **Genius Hours** and **Project-Based Learning.**

Source: From *Rigor by Design, Not Chance: Laying the Groundwork for Deeper Understanding,* by K. Hess, 2018, Educational Research in Action. Adapted with permission.

TEACHER TOOL 2

Developing Prompts and Scoring Criteria (Portfolio Defense)

Self-Direction Criteria	Collaboration Criteria	Applying Creative Thinking Criteria
SELF-AWARENESS Cite examples from your work to evaluate how you have expanded your strengths and interests by setting learning goals beyond assigned tasks.	**SELF-AWARENESS AND PERSONAL RESPONSIBILITY** Analyze how your roles and responsibilities within the group dynamics demonstrated individual responsibility and enhanced group equity.	**SELF-AWARENESS** Analyze how using creative problem-solving processes helped you pursue personal interests, seek out supportive resources or environments, or share ideas or products that positively affect others.
INITIATIVE AND OWNERSHIP In what ways did you seek input to help you analyze the content and context of learning tasks to reshape, extend, or enhance your learning?	**COMMUNICATING** Cite evidence showing that you contributed well-supported ideas and validated each team member's contributions with positive reinforcement and constructive feedback.	**TOLERATING RISK AND AMBIGUITY** Evaluate the effects of approaches used and decisions made throughout the creative process, and suggest how you might apply your learning or insights to challenge established social, cultural, or artistic norms.
GOAL SETTING AND PLANNING How did a project-based learning goal push your learning beyond the task, and how did you use feedback to improve the plan?	**DECISION MAKING AND PROBLEM SOLVING** How did you work with your group to evaluate the effects of decisions made to resolve conflicts in terms of honoring each member's contributions and strengthening group cohesiveness?	**CULTIVATING IDEAS** Describe how you were able to convey your interests, personal insights, or novel ideas in solving a challenge.
ENGAGING AND MANAGING Provide examples of how you set and maintained a high standard of work quality and how you plan to improve your learning processes in the future.	**CONTRIBUTING AND SUPPORTING** Describe how you analyzed alternative approaches that increased your personal learning or advanced the overall quality of your group's performance.	**EXPERIMENTING AND VALIDATING** Analyze alternative approaches that could have improved the application of your personal insights or advanced the overall quality of the final product (clarity, effectiveness, or uniqueness).
MONITORING AND ADAPTING Analyze your learning by citing examples of how you met or exceeded project goals, transformed mistakes into new learning, or enhanced your personal growth.	**MONITORING AND ADAPTING** Describe how you worked with your group to reflect on progress and adapt group norms, roles, or strategies to optimize the collective group effort and enhance a positive group dynamic.	**MONITORING AND ADAPTING** Use examples from this project to evaluate how solving a personally meaningful challenge can help you in future challenges.

Source: From *Toolkits & Resources*, by BEST for the Future, 2022. https://best-future.org/resources/. Adapted with permission.

References

Almarode, J. (2018, February). 8 ways to increase engagement with your students. Corwin Connect. https://corwin-connect.com/2018/02/8-ways-increase-engagement-students/

Anderson, L., Krathwohl, D., Airasian, P., Cruikshank, K., Mayer, R., Pintrich, P., Raths, J., & Wittrock, M. (Eds.). (2001). *A taxonomy for learning, teaching, and assessing: A revision of Bloom's taxonomy of educational objectives.* Addison Wesley Longman.

Beers, K., & Probst, R. (2013). *Notice and note: Strategies for close reading.* Heinemann.

Berry, A. (2020). Disrupting to driving: Exploring upper primary teachers' perspectives on student engagement. *Teachers and Teaching, 26*(2), 145–165.

BEST for the Future. (2022). *Toolkits & resources.* https://www.best-future.org/resources/

Black, P., & Wiliam, D. (1998, October). Inside the black box: Raising standards through classroom assessment. *Phi Delta Kappan, 80*(2), 139–148.

Bloom, B. S. (Ed.), Englehardt, M. D., Furst, E. J., Hill, W. H., & Krathwohl, D. R. (1956). *The taxonomy of educational objectives, Book 1: Cognitive domain.* David McKay Company.

Brady-Myerov, M. (2019, October). Classroom podcasting for the middle grades. MiddleWeb. https://www.middleweb.com/41246/classroom-podcasting-for-the-middle-grades/

Briceño, E. (2015, November). Mistakes are not all created equal. Mindset Works. https://community.mindsetworks.com/entry/mistakes-are-not-all-created-equal

Brown, P., Roediger, H. L., & McDaniel, M. A. (2014). *Make it stick: The science of successful learning.* Belnap Press.

Byrne, R. (2021, September). Mind maps versus concept maps and a bunch of tools for both. Practical Ed Tech. https://practicaledtech.com/2021/09/22/mind-maps-vs-concept-maps-and-a-bunch-of-tools-for-both/

Calderón, M. (2011). *Teaching reading and comprehension to English learners K–5.* Solution Tree Press.

Colorín Colorado. (2007). Using cognates to develop comprehension in English. http://www.colorincolorado.org/article/using-cognates-develop-comprehension-english

Commins, N. (2011). Meaning is everything: Comprehension work with English language learners. In H. Daniels (Ed.), *Comprehension going forward* (pp. 192–214). Heinemann.

Donohoo, J., & Hite, S. (2021). Addressing inequity with the power of collective efficacy. *Educational Leadership, 78*(6). https://www.ascd.org/el/articles/addressing-inequity-with-the-power-of-collective-efficacy

Duckworth, A. L., Peterson, C., Matthews, M., & Kelly, D. (2007). Grit: Perseverance and passion for long-term goals. *Journal of Personality and Social Psychology, 92*(6), 1087–1101.

Farah, K. (2020). Everything you need to know about building a great screencast video. Cult of Pedagogy. https://www.cultofpedagogy.com/screencast-videos/

Farrington, C. A., Roderick, M., Allensworth, E., Nagaoka, J., Keyes, T. S., Johnson, D. W., & Beechum, N. O. (2012). *Teaching adolescents to become learners: The role of non-cognitive factors in shaping school performance: A critical literature review.* University of Chicago Consortium on Chicago School Research.

Frey, N., & Fisher, D. (2021). New thinking about student engagement. *Educational Leadership, 79*(4). https://www.ascd.org/el/articles/show-and-tell-a-video-column-new-thinking-about-student-engagement

Frey, N., Hattie, J., & Fisher, D. (2018). *Developing assessment-capable learners, grades K–12.* Corwin.

Gibbons, P. (2009). *English learners, academic literacy, and thinking.* Heinemann.

Goodwin, B. (2017). Helping students develop schemas. *Educational Leadership, 75*(2), 81–82.

Goudvis, A., Harvey, S., Buhrow, B., & Upczak-Garcia, A. (2012). *Scaffolding: The comprehension toolkit for English language learners.* Heinemann.

Harris, J., Ainscow, M., Spina, N., & Carrington, S. (2017, September). Opinion: The value of "slow schools." https://www.theeducatoronline.com/k12/news/opinion-the-value-of-slow-schools/241138

Hattie, J. (2009). *Visible learning: A synthesis of over 800 meta-analyses relating to achievement.* Routledge.

Hattie, J. (2012). *Visible learning for teachers: Maximizing impact on learning.* Routledge.

Hellerich, K. (2021, September 8). An exercise in digital storytelling. Edutopia. https://www.edutopia.org/article/exercise-digital-storytelling

Hess, K. (1985). *Enhancing writing through imagery.* Royal Fireworks Press.

Hess, K. (2013). *Linking research with practice: A local assessment toolkit to guide school leaders.* Educational Research in Action.

Hess, K. (2018a). *A local assessment toolkit to promote deeper learning: Transforming research into practice.* Corwin.

Hess, K. (2018b). *Rigor by design, not chance: Laying the foundation for deeper understanding.* Educational Research in Action.

Hess, K. (2021). *The rigor by design playbook: The what, the why, and the how.* Educational Research in Action.

Hess, K., Carlock, D., Jones, B., & Walkup, J. (2009). *What exactly do "fewer, clearer, and higher standards" really look like in the classroom? Using a cognitive rigor matrix to analyze curriculum, plan lessons, and implement assessments.* https://www.karin-hess.com/_files/ugd/5e86bd_2f72d4acd00a4494b0677adecafd119f.pdf

Hess, K., Gong, B. & Steinitz, R. (2014). *Ready for college and career? Achieving the Common Core Standards and beyond through deeper, student-centered learning.* Nellie Mae Education Foundation. https://www.nmefoundation.org/wp-content/uploads/2020/05/Ready-for-College-and-Career.pdf

Hewlett Foundation. (2013). *Deeper learning competencies.* https://hewlett.org/wp-content/uploads/2016/08/Deeper_Learning_Defined__April_2013.pdf

Huynh, T. (2022, February 16). Planning our lessons: Forest, trees, leaves. MiddleWeb. https://www.middleweb.com/46595/planning-our-lessons-forest-trees-leaves/

Jackson, T. (2021). How productive failure can support learning in novel problem-solving. *Academia Letters*. https://doi.org/10.20935/AL3887

Johnson, D., & Johnson, R. (1975). *Learning together and alone: Cooperative, competitive, and individualistic learning*. Prentice-Hall.

Kagan, S. (1992). *Cooperative learning*. Resources for Teachers.

Keeley, P., Eberle, F., & Dorsey, C. (2008). *Uncovering student ideas in science, Vol. 3: Another 25 formative assessment probes*. NSTA Press.

Krulder, J. (2018, March 6). 5-minute writing conferences. Edutopia. https://www.edutopia.org/article/5-minute-writing-conferences

Krulder, J. (2020, November 2). Supporting choice reading for students in distance learning. Edutopia. https://www.edutopia.org/article/supporting-choice-reading-students-distance-learning

LaVogue, T. (2020, February 3). Why I scrum: Using a project management tool for PBL. PBL Works. https://www.pblworks.org/blog/why-i-scrum-using-project-management-tool-pbl

Lench, S., Fukuda, E., & Anderson, R. (2015). *Essential skills and dispositions: Developmental frameworks for collaboration, communication, creativity, and self-direction*. Educational Policy Improvement Center. https://www.inflexion.org/essential-skills-and-dispositions-development-frameworks/

Love, S., & Strobaugh, R. (2018). *Critical thinking in the classroom: A practitioner's guide*. Mentoring Minds.

Lundgren, C., & Willner, L. S. (2021). Putting discourse first. *MinneTESOL Journal, 37*(1).

McTighe, J., & Wiggins, G. (2013). *Essential questions: Opening doors to student understanding*. ASCD.

Newell, A., & Simon, H. (1972). *Human problem-solving*. Prentice Hall.

Newmann, F., King, M., & Carmichael, D. (2007). *Authentic instruction and assessment: Common standards for rigor and relevance in teaching academic subjects*. Iowa Department of Education. http://psdsped.pbworks.com/w/file/fetch/67042713/Authentic-Instruction-Assessment-BlueBook.pdf

Oakley, B., Rogowsky, B., & Sejnowski, T. (2021). *Uncommon sense teaching: Practical insights in brain science to help students learn*. TarcherPerigee.

Paige, D. D., Sizemore, J. M., & Neace, W. P. (2013, January 28). Working inside the box: Exploring the relationship between student engagement and cognitive rigor. *NASSP Bulletin, 97*, 105–123.

Pellegrino, J., & Hilton, M. (Eds.). (2012). *Education for life and work: Developing transferable knowledge and skills in the 21st century*. National Academies Press.

Perkins, D. (1984). Creativity by design. *Educational Leadership, 42*(1), 18–25.

Rowe, M. B. (1986). Wait time: Slowing down may be a way of speeding up! *Journal of Teacher Education, 37*(1), 43–50. https://doi.org/10.1177/002248718603700110

Savitz-Romer, M., & Bouffard, S. (2012). *Ready, willing, and able: A developmental approach to college access and success*. Harvard Education Press.

Smith, A. (2017). Writing driving questions [Video]. YouTube. https://www.youtube.com/watch?v=u0Eojnkb3Gs.

Sousa, D. A. (2015). *Brain-friendly assessments: What they are and how to use them*. Learning Sciences International.

Sousa, D. A. (2022). *How the brain learns* (6th ed.). Corwin.

Spencer, J. (2015, October). The 20-minute peer feedback system. https://spencerauthor.com/the-20-minute-peer-feedback-system/

Spencer, J. (2020, May). Seven reasons to pilot genius hour projects. https://spencerauthor.com/reasons-for-genius-hour/

Sriram, R. (2020, April 13). The neuroscience behind productive struggle. Edutopia. https://www.edutopia.org/article/neuroscience-behind-productive-struggle

Stone, A. (2022, January). Creating video guides to prepare students for science labs. Edutopia. https://www.edutopia.org/article/creating-video-guides-prepare-students-science-labs

Surowiecki, J. (2005). *The wisdom of crowds: Why the many are smarter than the few and how collective wisdom shapes business, economics, societies, and nations.* Anchor Books.

Teaching Channel. (n.d.) The art of questioning: Content, meaning, and style. [Video]. https://learn.teachingchannel.com/video/structuring-questioning-in-classroom

Vygotsky, L. S. (1978). *Mind and society: The development of higher mental processes.* Harvard University Press.

Webb, N. (1997). Research Monograph Number 6: Criteria for alignment of expectations and assessments on mathematics and science education. CCSSO.

WIDA. (2020). *WIDA English language development standards framework, 2020 edition: Kindergarten–grade 12.* WIDA. https://wida.wisc.edu/teach/standards/eld

Wiggins, G., & McTighe, J. (2005). *Understanding by design* (2nd ed.). ASCD.

Wiliam, D. (2015). Designing great hinge questions. *Educational Leadership, 73*(1), 40–44.

Willis, J. (2021, December 10). Six tips for developing students' executive functioning skills. https://www.ascd.org/blogs/six-tips-for-developing-students-executive-functioning-skills

Wilson, D., & Conyers, M. (2015, April). Strategies for strengthening the brain's executive functions. Edutopia. http://www.edutopia.org/blog/strategies-strengthening-brains-executive-functions-donna-wilson-marcus-conyers

Wise, M., & McTighe, J. (2017, October). Middle schoolers go global. *Educational Leadership, 75*(2), 12–18.

Index

The letter *f* following a page locator denotes a figure. Tools and activities are capitalized.

About the Author

Karin Hess, EdD, is founder and president of Educational Research in Action and author of the Hess Cognitive Rigor Matrices. She is a former classroom teacher and school administrator with more than 40 years of experience in curriculum, instruction, and assessment. She is an internationally recognized leader in applying the concepts of cognitive rigor, depth of knowledge, and learning progressions to the design and development of state and school-based curriculum and assessment systems. An expert in multiple content areas, she specializes in the design and use of performance-based assessments for preK–12 students.

At the Center for Assessment in Dover, New Hampshire, Hess led the development of multistate K–12 standards and designed general and special education large-scale state assessments. Previously, she worked as New Jersey's state director for gifted education, a program evaluator for the Vermont Mathematics Project, and a developer and editor of K–8 performance tasks for *Science Exemplars* (www.exemplars.com). She has provided technical expertise to EL Education, Renaissance Learning, the Mathematics Advisory Team for Achieve3000, the Critical Thinking Advisory Team for Mentoring Minds, and the World-Class Instructional Design and Assessment (WIDA) consortium in revising the 2020 English Language Development Standards Framework.

Hess has authored or coauthored more than a dozen books in the field of education. Her most recent work includes *A Local Assessment Toolkit to Promote Deeper Learning: Transforming Research into Practice* (Corwin, 2018); codeveloping Benchmark Education's *Ready to Advance* curriculum for prekindergarten (2019); and coauthoring, with Rose Colby and Dan Joseph, *Deeper Competency-Based Learning: Making Equitable, Student-Centered, Sustainable Shifts* (Corwin, 2020).

In her work with schools, Hess provides practical, classroom-tested tools and in-depth guidance for implementing competency-based educational systems and strategies to enhance deeper learning for every student.